DECCA STUDIOS AND KLOOKS KLEEK

WEST HAMPSTEAD'S MUSICAL HERITAGE REMEMBERED

DICK WEINDLING &
MARIANNE COLLOMS

Cover image credits:

Graham Bond Organisation (Courtesy of Jon Hiseman); Dick Jordan, Harrison Marks and Jackie Salt (Courtesy of Dick Jordan); Django Reinhardt (Courtesy of American Memory at the Library of Congress, William Gottlieb, 1946, LC-GLB23-0730 DLC); Mike Martin Band (Courtesy of Dick Jordan); Mick Jagger (Courtesy of Gonzalo Andrés); Eric Clapton (Courtesy of Matt Gibbons); Zoot and Big Roll Band (Courtesy of Zoot Money); The Beatles with Pete Best (Courtesy of Joe Flannery, from his book *Standing in the Wings: The Beatles, Brian Epstein and Me*); Dick Heckstall-Smith (Courtesy of Dick Jordan); Tom Jones (Courtesy of Georgio); Geoff Williams (Courtesy of Dick Jordan); David Bowie (Courtesy of Jorge Barrios)

First published 2013

The History Press
The Mill, Brimscombe Port
Stroud, Gloucestershire, GL5 2QG
www.thehistorypress.co.uk

British Library Cataloguing in Publication Data.
A catalogue record for this book is available from the British Library.

ISBN 978 0 7509 5287 3

Typesetting and origination by The History Press
Printed in Great Britain

CONTENTS

ACKNOWLEDGEMENTS

We would like to thank Dick Jordan and Geoff Williams without whom we could not have written the chapter about Klooks Kleek. Thanks also to Jon Hiseman and Colin Richardson for helping us to contact Dick Jordan.

Other people who have contributed with their memories of Decca and Klooks are:

Denise Barrett
Pat Boland
Gordon Chamley
Roger Dean
Laurie Fincham
Keef Hartley
Pauline Hurley
Dave Humphries
Ric Lee
Patrick Linnane
Henry Lowther
Leo Lyons
Zoot Money
Andrew Loog Oldham
Roger Pettet
Val Simmonds
Neil Slavin
Paul Soper
George Underwood
Derek Varnals
Mike Vernon
Chris Welch
Mel West
Adrian Wyatt

INTRODUCTION

This is a history of Decca Studios in Broadhurst Gardens West Hampstead, in a building which began life as West Hampstead Town Hall. It is also the story of Klooks Kleek, a jazz and blues club, situated in the Railway Hotel, the pub next door to Decca.

The first chapter looks at the Crystalate Record Company which Decca bought in 1937. They moved into Crystalate's studio in Broadhurst Gardens which then became Decca's main recording facility until 1981. Currently the whole building is being used by the English National Opera and their archivist, Clare Colvin, said they acquired it on 27 November 1981.

The second chapter looks at the development of the Railway Hotel and West Hampstead Town Hall, which was built for private functions not as a municipal Town Hall.

The third chapter provides the history of Klooks Kleek, which was a major venue for jazz and the evolving British blues scene. During the ten years from 1961 to 1970, when the club ran, some of the most famous names in jazz and blues played there.

1

DECCA STUDIOS

The Decca Studios building was previously West Hampstead Town Hall, bought by the Crystalate Record Company in 1928. This became Decca Studios in 1937. In its final form, the building housed three studios. Studio One was straight ahead as you entered the building with an upstairs control room, Studio Two was downstairs, and the very large Studio Three, built in the 1960s, was down a long corridor towards the back of the building.

Decca Studios, now English National Opera.

Crystalate

In August 1901 the Crystalate Company was founded at Golden Green (note, not Golders Green), Haddow, near Tunbridge in Kent, by a partnership of a London and an American firm. The British company had begun by introducing colours into minerals and making imitation ivory. The American company produced billiard balls and poker chips, before moving on to making gramophone records from shellac. In July 1901 the American director, George Henry Burt (1863–?), applied for a trademark on the word 'Crystalate' to cover all their plastic products. The secret formula to make Crystalate substances was kept in a sealed iron box which required two keys to open it: Burt had one and Percy Warnford-Davis (1856–1919), the English director, had the other. It is said that they made the first records to be pressed in England in 1901/2; but there is no direct evidence of this apart from the 1922 recollections of Charles Davis, the works manager.

The company made records for a large number of the very early labels, such as Zonophone and Berliner. After Burt left Crystalate in 1907 the company was run by the Warnford-Davis family with Darryll Warnford-Davis becoming chairman after the death of his father Percy in 1919. New contracts followed, for example with Imperial Records. Initially imported from America, Crystalate took over their manufacture from 1923 to 1934. Between these dates they produced over 2,100 different titles. In 1926 the company moved their office and recording studio from No. 63 Farrington Road to No. 69, Imperial House. In 1929 they moved again to Nos 60–62 City Road, which they called Crystalate House. A very productive period followed, during which time Crystalate produced large numbers of records for labels including Eclipse and Crown for Woolworths. They also made Victory records from 1928, which were sold in Woolworths for 6*d* (for more information see 'The History of the Crystalate Company' by Frank Andrews, *Hillandale News*, Vols 134, 135, 136, 1983 and 1984).

The British Pathé website has a short film, *Making a Record 1918-1924*, which shows how a recording was made and a record pressed.

Rex records were begun in 1933 and made by Crystalate. At first they cost a shilling which represented very good value for enormously popular artists of the day such as Gracie Fields, Larry Adler, Billy Cotton and Sandy Powell. Also on the label were the American stars Bing Crosby, the Mills Brothers, the Boswell Sisters, and Cab Calloway. Between 1933 and their demise in 1948, over 2,200 Rex titles were produced (*Beltona* by Bill Dean-Myatt, 2007).

Crystalate took over West Hampstead Town Hall in 1928 and moved their recording studio there. That year the Crystalate Manufacturing Company appeared at No. 165 Broadhurst Gardens for the first time in the phone book. A prospectus was published in *The Times* on 2 February 1928, which announced that, 'West Hampstead Town Hall has recently been purchased and equipped as a modern recording studio'.

Arthur Haddy (1906-1989) was a brilliant young engineer working with the Western Electric Company. On an audio recording at the British Library, made by him in 1983, he tells how he was engaged to Lilian, the daughter of the popular comic singer Harry Fay (real name Henry Fahey). Born in Liverpool in 1878, Fay started out performing in the music halls and then had a very successful recording career. The Zonophone catalogue for 1913/14 lists over fifty of his records, including the well-known songs 'Has Anybody Here Seen Kelly?', 'Boiled Beef and Carrots', 'I Do Like to be Beside the Seaside', and 'Let's All Go Down the Strand'. During the First World War, Harry had a huge hit with 'It's a Long Way to Tipperary'.

In 1929, Arthur Haddy accompanied Harry Fay to a recording session at the Crystalate studio in Broadhurst Gardens. Electric recording had just begun and Haddy wasn't impressed with what he saw there, calling it 'a load of junk'. He jokingly said, 'I think I could make a better lot of it on the kitchen table.' Less than six months later Harry Fay phoned him and said the managing director of Crystalate wanted to see him. Haddy met Darryll Warnford-Davis, who asked him if he'd meant what he said about making better equipment. Haddy explained he'd been joking but was willing to try. In the next few months he made an amplifier and a record-cutting head and took them to the studio for a trial. The Crystalate engineers were very impressed with Haddy's equipment, which produced better results than anything being imported from America. Warnford-Davis wanted Haddy to join Crystalate and offered him double his present salary, which at first he refused, preferring to stay at the prestigious Western Electric Company. But then, as Haddy laughingly says, 'My future wife said no bigger salary, no engagement!' So he moved to Crystalate and brought his new equipment to the Broadhurst Gardens studio. The increase in salary clearly worked and Arthur and Lilian Fahey were married in 1930.

CRYSTALATE ARTISTS

Haddy remembers some of the people he recorded at the Crystalate studio. We are fortunate that many of these early recordings are now available on YouTube.

Jay Whidden

James 'Jay' Whidden was born in Livingstone, Montana, about 1890. He was a violinist and band leader who came to England in 1912. He was very fond of recounting his days as a cowboy, saying the frostbitten fingertips on his left hand had been removed by the simple expedient of his cattleman father who amputated them with a knife.

Jay's family moved to New York, where his father worked in the docks and Jay began to learn the violin after hearing his father play Irish jigs. He became fascinated by Ragtime music, which was very popular in the first decade of the twentieth century. With his friend and co-writer Con Conrad, Jay wrote several Ragtime songs, two of which were put on in the Ziegfeld Follies of 1912. Ragtime spread to England and Con and Jay decided to pool their money and sail by tramp steamer to London. They became the Ragtime Duo and appeared in the show *Everybody's Doing It*, which was based on Irving Berlin's words and music. They made their debut in January 1913 and received very good press notices as 'real' American and 'real' Ragtime performers.

Based on their success, they brought over an American musical comedy called *The Honeymoon Express*, complete with special effects of a famous chase between an automobile and train, which was literally done with smoke and mirrors. The show opened at the Oxford Theatre of Varieties on the corner of Oxford Street and Tottenham Court Road in April 1913. It had a successful run and went on tour. Con returned to America in 1916 and achieved worldwide success with his songs, such as 'Ma, He's Makin' Eyes At Me'.

Jay appeared several times, with another partner, at the London Palladium during the First World War and he continued his song-writing career. In 1925 he was employed as musical director for the Gordon Group Hotels, which included the prestigious Hotel Metropole just off Trafalgar Square – the British Pathé website has a clip of him performing there in 1926. Jay recruited some of the best British musicians for his Midnight Follies dance band and they began regular broadcasts on the BBC in December 1925. This led to great success and Whidden made his first record for Columbia records in March 1926. He went on to sign a contract with Crystalate to appear on its Imperial and Victory labels, and his first recordings were done in August 1928.

His 1930 recording of the wonderful 'Happy Feet', made in Broadhurst Gardens, can be heard on YouTube. Whidden later recorded for several other companies and his popularity continued on into the Second World War.

Sandy Powell

This very popular comedian was born in Rotherdam in 1900 as Albert Arthur Powell. His father nicknamed him 'Sandy' on account of his ginger hair and the name obviously stuck. His radio work during the 1930s made him a household name and his catchphrase 'Can you hear me, Mother?' was much parroted. Apparently this expression originated from the fact that his mother was indeed hard of hearing and when, during a show, Sandy dropped his lines, he used the phrase to comic effect while reorganising his script. Once the expression caught on he always introduced his radio shows with the words 'Can you hear me, Mother?'

In addition to these radio shows Sandy started producing records, several in collaboration with Gracie Fields. His lyrics were based around different trades and occupations, including a dentist, fireman, policeman and several others (some of which can be seen on YouTube). 'The Lost Policeman', the first in this series, sold half a million copies. Recorded at the Crystalate studios on the cheap Broadcast label it sold so successfully that Sandy continued to record for Broadcast and Rex and, between 1929 (the date of the 'The Lost Policeman' recording) and 1942, he completed a total of eighty-five records.

In addition to his radio work, and in-between producing records, Sandy acted in a number of films and appeared on television and in pantomimes. One of his favoured acts was ventriloquism, during which his animated dummy would often fall apart. In 1975 he was awarded an MBE and he continued to perform up until his death in 1982. There is a DVD of his sketches, entitled, as you might guess, *Can You Hear Me Mother?*

Charles Penrose, 'The Laughing Policeman'

Charles Penrose (1873-1952) has been known by a number of names in his time. Born as Frank Penrose Cawse, in Biggleswade, Bedfordshire, his parents decided against the name Frank and re-registered him as Charles Penrose Dunar Cawse not long after his birth. Charles would go on to call himself Charles Jolly at the time of his recording of the much-loved 'The Laughing Policeman'.

Although his early career saw him follow his father into the jewellery trade, Charles eventually became an entertainer, a theatre performer at the West End and a radio comedian. Charles recorded a number of songs in the 'Laughing' series, including 'The Laughing Lover', 'The Laughing Curate' and 'The Laughing Major'. He is best known, however, for his amusing song 'The Laughing Policeman', which he recorded in the 1920s. This track remained a popular favourite well into the 1970s and was a frequent request on the BBC's *Children's Favourites*.

Master Joe Peterson

Master Joe Peterson signed with Crystalate in 1933 aged 20. But Master Joe was really a woman called Mary O'Rourke, who was born in Helensburgh, Scotland. She was brought up in Glasgow in an Irish show business family, and was the twelfth of fourteen children. With a unique and beautiful voice she won talent contests and was recruited by her uncle to take the place of his boy singers whose voices broke in adolescence. Her uncle, the Cockney entertainer and impresario Ted Stebbings, taught her how to impersonate a boy's voice in song. She performed in the music halls and had a successful recording career, releasing nearly sixty songs on the Rex label between 1934 and 1942.

Despite her popularity, the BBC refused to let Mary broadcast as Master Joe because they considered her 'improper' for dressing as a boy, complete with her trademark Eton collar.

She tried to overcome the label of a boy singer and record under her own name but was dissuaded by her uncle. After an unhappy marriage she began to drink heavily. Although her last record was released in 1942 she continued performing throughout the 1950s and even appeared on Scottish television as Master Joe in 1963, aged 50. She died in 1964.

Vera Lynn

Vera Lynn is perhaps best known for being the Forces Sweetheart during the Second World War but she had began her singing career much earlier. She worked with the very popular dance bands of Joe Loss and Charlie Kuntz and made her first solo recordings for Crystalate's Crown label in 1936. Later, she recorded on their Rex label.

She made an impact on a young Dirk Bogarde. Born in 1921 and brought up near the studios at 173 Goldhurst Terrace, Dirk was sent to Glasgow when he was 13 to live with his aunt and uncle. This was an unhappy three or four years for him, but he found a refuge in Woolworths. He writes in his autobiography, *A Postillion Struck by Lightning* (1986):

> Woolworth's was my usual haven. Because it was warm and bright, and filled with people. Here was Life ... Music played all day. The record counter had a constant supply of melody. To the lingering refrains of 'When The Poppies Bloom Again' I would sit on a high stool eating a Chocolate Fudge Ice Cream and beam happily at the world about me. Guiltless. It was all heady stuff.

Vera Lynn recorded 'When the Poppies Bloom Again' at Broadhurst Gardens for Crystalate in 1936.

During the Depression many of the record companies ran into financial trouble and were bought up by either EMI or Decca. In March 1937 the record division of Crystalate was sold to Decca for £200,000 (*The Times*, 2 March 1937). Haddy and his colleague Kenneth 'Wilkie' Wilkinson (1912–2004) were worried they'd soon be paid off because Decca had their own studio in Upper Thames Street and didn't need the Broadhurst Gardens one as well. He remembers that they were recording Master Joe Peterson and the record was a big hit, recalling that they 'lived on it for nine months'. Then they heard that Mr Lewis (Edward Lewis, the Director of Decca), had decided to close the studio in Thames Street instead and move all the recording to Broadhurst Gardens. Haddy said that they were so enthusiastic that they worked until four o'clock in the morning just for the love of it. Edward Lewis said to Haddy that Warnford-Davis had told him that he got a bargain when he bought Crystalate, but he got an even bigger bargain with 'young Haddy from Hampstead' (Arthur Haddy interviewed by Laurence Stapley, *Oral History of Recorded Sound*, 5 December 1983, British Library: C90/16/01).

DECCA AND SIR EDWARD LEWIS

Origins

The origins of Decca go back to a company called Barnett Samuel and Sons which was established by Barnett Samuel, a naturalised Russian immigrant in 1832. They started out producing tortoiseshell doorknobs, combs and knife handles in Sheffield, but moved to London as the music industry expanded, making and selling banjos. By 1878 they were at No. 32 Worship Street, Finsbury Square. Barnett died in 1882 but the company carried on, led by his son Nelson and a nephew called Max Samuel. In 1901 they were one of the largest musical instrument wholesalers in the country and they had their own piano factory in North London. In 1914 they patented a portable gramophone called the Decca Dulcephone. Many of these machines were used by soldiers in the trenches during the First World War. After the war, sales of the portable gramophone increased and this became the main product manufactured by the company.

The Decca Name

In his 1956 autobiography, Edward Lewis said that nobody knew the origin of the word 'Decca'. In a 1981 article for the magazine *Sounds*, Brian Rust, an authority on early records, agreed with Lewis, but noted much later that there was a Sunday radio programme during the 1930s which used a call sign played on tubular bells or a vibraphone; the five notes played being D, E, C, C, A. He also noted that the latest records from Decca were played in the programme. This fits in with the original Decca logo which was a musical stave with the notes D, E, C, C, A, written in crotchets with the letters noted underneath. More recently (in 1988) Edgar Samuel says he was told about the trademark by Wilfred S. Barnett of the original company. In 1914, when Barnett Samuel and Sons produced their portable gramophone, they wanted a word for their exports which could be easily recognised and have the same pronunciation in different languages, so Wilfred Barnett merged the word Mecca with the initial D of their trademark Dulcephone to produce the word Decca.

Expansion of Decca

The story of Decca's growth and success is really the story of Edward Lewis (1900–1980), a young stockbroker from Derby. In the summer of 1928 Lewis received a telegram while he was on holiday in France, asking if he would be interested in the stock market floatation of Barnett Samuel and Sons. He agreed, and by the end of September 1928 he was the broker of the newly named Decca Gramophone Company. The Samuel family sold out completely. Lewis then suggested the idea of making records to the directors of the new company but they turned it down. So, in January 1929, Lewis decided to form a syndicate called Malden Holdings to buy the ailing Duophone factory at Shannon Corner on the Kingston bypass for £145,000 (equivalent today to about £6.6 million). He also bought out Decca and, when their shares were issued on 28 February 1929, they were oversubscribed twice over. As Lewis said, the success of their portable gramophone meant there was 'magic in the word Decca'. Lewis became the managing director, but the new company was soon engulfed in the Depression – which began with the Wall Street crash – later that year. Lewis faced a titanic struggle to prevent Decca going under, a struggle that lasted a decade. Within a year of the 1929 share issue, Decca's bankers were threatening foreclosure, and at its financial nadir some years later, the company even had its telephone cut off.

Despite knowing little about the music business, Lewis was the genius who made Decca one of the largest record companies in the world. The first records appeared in July 1929 and were recorded in the Decca studio at the Chenil Galleries on King's Road, Chelsea. Early recordings were made with the Billy Cotton and Ambrose dance bands. One of Lewis's first decisions was to drop the price of records to 1*s* 6*d* in 1931, to undercut the other companies. The same year his big coup was to sign the most popular dance bandleader of the time, Jack Hylton. As part of the deal, Hylton asked for, and was given, 40,000 Decca shares; it proved a sound investment for Lewis, as Hylton's first record for Decca, 'Rhymes', sold 300,000 copies. Part of its popularity was the catchy sing-along line, 'That was a cute little rhyme, Sing us another one do'. In 1932 Lewis bought the British rights for the American label Brunswick at a cost of £15,000 (about £780,000 today). Then in August 1934 Lewis launched US Decca from their offices in New York's famous Flatiron Building. The key Decca man in New York was Jack Kapp, a Brunswick executive, who brought in the best-selling artists Bing Crosby, Louis Armstrong, the Boswell Sisters, Guy Lombardo and the Mills Brothers.

In 1933, Decca left Chelsea and moved their studios to a former City of London Brewery at No. 89 Upper Thames Street, near St Paul's Cathedral. But this was not ideal, because the studio was not on the ground floor so when a grand piano was needed it had to be lifted in by crane.

Lewis Acquires Crystalate

In his autobiography, Lewis said that in 1937 Crystalate, 'had found the going rougher and rougher'. Due to changes in the price of Woolworths, HMV and Columbia records, their financial situation became serious. In March 1937 Lewis bought Crystalate for £200,000 (today worth about £10 million), and through this Decca obtained the budget Rex record label and the studios in Broadhurst Gardens. It was soon decided that the facilities here were better and more convenient than at Upper Thames Street, and so Broadhurst Gardens became Decca Studios.

In May 1937, after two years of discussion, Decca and their rival EMI joint-purchased British Homophone's masters for £22,500 (about £1 million today). This company, which produced the Sterno label only available through Marks & Spencer, had a factory and office in the Kilburn High Road. The most important artist on the Sterno label was the pianist Charlie Kunz who had sold an astonishing 1 million records. At the time, he was the highest paid pianist in the world, earning £1,000 week. Born in America, Kunz lived in Willesden.

In September 1937 the price of Decca's 1*s* 6*d* records was increased to 2*s*, but Lewis held the Rex label at 1*s* 6*d*. By 1939, Decca and EMI had between them bought up all the other record companies in England, leaving the two companies as rival giants.

An interesting history of the early recording companies in England and America is given in Louis Barfe's 2004 book, *Where Have All the Good Times Gone? The Rise and Fall of the Record Industries.*

A search of the Ancestry phone books shows that from at least 1934 Edward Lewis lived at Heath View, Heathbrow, near the Jack Straw's Castle pub. However, in 1941 his house was destroyed by a parachute landmine, though nobody was injured. He moved to the other side of the Whitestone Pond and lived in a flat, No. 2 Bellmoor, until about 1957. In later life he had a London home at No. 69a Cadogan Place, Chelsea, and his country house was Bridge House Farm in Felsted, Essex. Lewis was knighted in 1951 and died in January 1980, when Decca was taken over by the Dutch company Polygram. Lewis left an estate of £1,104,730.

Technical Advancements

Decca made a number of vital technological developments during the Second World War. In 1943 the company developed Decca Navigation, a form of direction finder, where multiple land-based transmitters broadcast radio signals to aircraft and ships. It became operational in January 1944 and was crucial to the Allies' success during the D-Day landings. The company was also asked by the government to develop a method of detecting German submarines from their engine noise. At Broadhurst Gardens, Arthur Haddy and the Decca team developed an enhanced low-frequency range detector. This was used by Coastal Command to track submarines and then guide aircraft to depth charge the enemy. After the war the technology was used to produce better sounding, wider frequency range 78rpm records labelled FFRR (Full Frequency Range Recording). Francis Attwood, Decca's advertising manager, suggested a trademark with the letters FFRR exiting a human ear, and this first appeared in the Gramophone magazine of

July 1945. Edward Lewis said the design was of immense value and illustrated the superiority of Decca recording. The FFRR technique led to the noted realism of Decca's classical recordings. It was then that it was applied to the pop side, with artists such as Mantovani, Charlie Kunz and Ted Heath. The British Pathé website has film showing the Duke of Edinburgh accompanied by Ted Lewis, visiting the Decca Navigator factory in 1957.

The LP

The Long-Playing record was launched in America in 1948 by Columbia Records. The new records were made of unplasticised vinyl (the old discs were made of brittle shellac). It enabled recordings to play for twenty to thirty-five minutes per side at 33rpm, compared with the limited three minutes playing time of existing 78rpm records. Decca was quick to use the LP for their recordings, which first appeared in June 1950. This gave them a considerable advantage over EMI, who stayed with the older format until October 1952. However, both companies continued to issue 78s until February 1960, as so many 78rpm gramophones had been sold. The British Pathé 1957 film of the Royal visit includes a sequence showing an LP being pressed, and 'old fashioned' shellac records being destroyed.

Stereo

In 1954, Arthur Haddy, Roy Wallace and Kenneth Wilkinson developed the Decca tree, a stereo microphone recording system for big orchestras. This, and the unusually wide-frequency range used for recording was called FFSS, or Full Frequency Stereophonic Sound. The first Decca stereo recordings were made in May 1954, in Victoria Hall, Geneva. They were the first European record company to use stereo technology, only three months after RCA Victor began recording in stereo in the US. Initially the records were only released in 'mono', or single channel sound; the stereo versions were finally issued in the 1960s as part of the 'Stereo Treasury' series. Most of their competitors didn't adopt stereo until 1957.

Ron Simmonds, who played trumpet with the Ted Heath band, talked about the first experimental recordings in stereo before there were twin track stereo recorders:

> Turning up at Decca studios I found the whole of the brass section standing out in the street. Bert Ezard told me that the saxes were making their tracks first and we had to wait outside. This was all very new and exciting. However it was being done, it was obviously not being separated on the twin tracks properly, because when we went in to dub our parts, several wrong notes were discovered on the saxophone recording, and we had to go back out into the street while they did the whole thing over again.

(www.jazzprofessional.com)

Decca Recording Artists

Decca had a huge list of artists who recorded thousands of records at the Broadhurst Gardens studio between 1937 and 1981, when the studio closed. It is impossible to cover all of them and only a selection is given here to illustrate the range of music produced. Over the forty-year period the popular music recorded at Decca reflects changing trends.

Classical Music

Decca also produced a vast catalogue of classical music recordings but these are not covered in this book. For a complete discography of Decca classical recordings from 1928 to 2009 see Philip Stuart at www.charm.rhul.ac.uk.

JAZZ AND SWING IN 1930s AND 1940s

Django Reinhardt, Stephane Grappelli and the Hot Club of Paris

On 25 August 1938 a band consisting of Django Reinhardt (guitar), Stephane Grappelli (violin and piano), Joseph Reinhardt (guitar), Eugene Vees (guitar), Emmanuel Soudieux (bass), and Beryl Davies (vocal) recorded at Decca Studios. They did further recordings on 30 August and 1 and 10 September 1938. After the war, another recording session was done on 1 February 1946.

Jean Reinhardt was born in Belgium in 1910 into a Romany gypsy family. His nickname of 'Django' means 'I awake' in Romany. His family made cane furniture and he grew up on the outskirts of Paris. Django learned to play the banjo, guitar and violin, and by his early teens was able to make a living by playing. When he was 18, the caravan that he and his wife Florine lived in caught fire and he was badly injured. His right leg was paralysed and the third and fourth fingers of his left hand were badly burned. Doctors believed they needed to amputate his leg, but he refused

Django Reinhardt. (Courtesy of American Memory at the Library of Congress, William Gottlieb, 1946, LC-GLB23-0730 DLC)

to have the surgery; within a year he was able to walk again, with the aid of a cane. He learned how to play the guitar using just two fingers for the solos and the injured fingers for the chords. He discovered the jazz of Louis Armstrong during the 1930s and met violinist Stephane Grappelli in Paris, 1931. They formed the Quintette du Hot Club of Paris in 1934 and had a major influence on early jazz. The Quintette du Hot Club played at the State Cinema Kilburn on 22 August 1939 and was positively reviewed in the *Melody Maker.* Their tour was abruptly ended when war was declared on 3 September 1939 and Django immediately returned to Paris. Grappelli stayed in England for the duration of the war.

For a biography see Michael Dregni, 2004, *Django: The Life and Music of a Gypsy Legend.* For a discography and biography see Paul Vernon, 2003, *Jean 'Django' Reinhardt: A Contextual Bio-discography 1910-1953.*

Ken 'Snakehips' Johnson

'Snakehips Swing' was recorded at Decca on 22 September 1938. Johnson was Britain's only black swing bandleader. Kendrick Johnson was born in British Guiana in 1914. His father was a doctor and Ken was sent to a school in Marlow. He was taught to dance by an American choreographer and his dancing style earned him the nickname 'Snakehips'. He appeared in the 1934 film *Oh Daddy* as a dancer. That year he visited America and heard the great orchestras of Cab Calloway and Fletcher Henderson in Harlem, which inspired him to set up his own band in 1937. Originally called Ken Johnson and his Swing Orchestra it later became the West Indian Dance Orchestra and in 1941 it was the resident band at the Café de Paris in London. Ken was very handsome and charismatic and always dressed in white tie and tails. Following broadcasts of the band he gained considerable popularity, with over 3 million listeners on BBC Radio. He was one of thirty-four people killed at the Café de Paris during an air raid on 8 March 1941, when a bomb fell down an air shaft. Stephen Poliakoff used the story as the basis for his 2013 TV drama, *Dancing on the Edge*.

POPULAR MUSIC IN THE 1940s AND 50s

Ted Heath Band

Ted Heath (1902–1969) led the most successful post-war big band in Britain, recording numerous albums at Decca and selling over 20 million records.

Dick Jordan and Geoff Williams recalled a story of the Ted Heath band when it was recording at Decca Studios in the 1960s:

> As in many other walks of life, recordings were sometimes affected by the lateness or no-show of those who preferred to exercise their elbows on licensed premises. One person with that sort of reputation was a gifted trombonist who had spent several years in the Ted Heath band: successful years until Ted grew weary of his social habits and showed him the door. Help was, however, at hand in the shape of Peter Burman, a jazz entrepreneur/manager who persuaded Ted that the trombonist was a reformed character and exactly what Ted needed for a recording at Decca. Ted reluctantly agreed. On the day, the band was forced to start minus one member of the trombone section, but the missing person eventually arrived several hours late, full of apologies and - totally sober! He took his place in the section, the light flashed and recording began, or should have begun, with a few bars solo from our man. He was silent. Ted stopped the music and forcefully enquired why he had not played. A red-faced trombonist responded, 'Could you lend me a trombone, Ted?'

The Mantovani Orchestra

Originally from Venice, Annunzio Paolo Mantovani moved to England as a child. Interested in music from a young age he discovered the violin when he was 14 years old and fell in love with the sound. He studied at the Trinty College of Music and would go on to give prominent recitals all around the country. When war broke out, his popular orchestral pieces were frequently played on BBC radio and live performances were well-attended. Once peacetime came he focused on recording rather than performing live. The composer and accordionist Ronnie Binge, who had played with Mantovani's Triple Orchestra, helped him to develop the 'Mantovani Sound', which was formed of a cascading or 'tumbling' effect on the strings. His biggest hit, 'Charmaine', was recorded at Decca Studios on 6 March 1951 with the help of engineer Arthur Lilley. This record would go on to sell over a million copies. Mantovani's last recordings were made in the mid-1970s and he died in 1980. British Pathé has several clips of him performing in the 1930s and 1940s.

Chris Barber and Lonnie Donegan

Hugh Mendl was a Decca producer who loved jazz. He had heard the new trad bands, such as Chris Barber, at the 100 Club and was keen to record them. But Decca boss Edward Lewis did not see a market for jazz records in the 1950s. He said to Mendl, 'Give the boy a radiogram' as if this would impress Chris Barber and gain his loyalty to Decca. Mendl said, 'I think he already has one', knowing that Barber had a huge record collection. Reluctantly, Lewis said Mendl could try one session as long as it did not cost more than £35. Mendl booked back-to-back afternoon and evening sessions.

On 13 July 1954 Chris Barber's band – Barber (trombone), Pat Halcox (cornet), Monty Sunshine (clarinet), Lonnie Donegan (banjo, guitar and vocals), Jim Bray (bass), and Ron Bowden (drums) – came into the studio to record an album, with Mendl as the producer and Arthur Lilly as the engineer. By the evening only five tracks had been recorded. Mendl sent the band to the Railway Hotel next door. When they returned they jammed a track which was called 'Merrydown Rag', after the Merrydown cider they had drunk in the pub. Mendl then pointed out that they still didn't have enough tracks for an album. By 9.30 p.m. some of the band had left when Lonnie Donegan suggested they could do some skiffle. Donegan sang and played acoustic guitar, Chris Barber played bass and Beryl Bryden, a renowned jazz singer, played the washboard. Mendl was concerned and said to Barber, 'I don't want to be unkind, but you're a trombone player.' Chris replied, 'I've had three lessons from a classical bass player and I think I can get by.' They recorded 'Rock Island Line' and 'John Henry' in a few takes and finished by 10 p.m. Donegan later embellished the story, saying that Mendl didn't want to record the tracks so they did it in his absence while he had a tea break, which wasn't true. The album *New Orleans Joys* was released in January 1955. 'Merrydown Rag' was issued in December 1954 as a single to promote the album, and 'Bobby Shaftoe' was released in March 1955. Neither single entered the charts.

In October 1955, the film *The Blackboard Jungle* had teenagers jiving to 'Rock Around the Clock' by Bill Haley and the Comets which topped the charts by the end of the month. Someone at Decca saw the teenage trend and it was decided to release 'Rock Island Line' as a single in November 1955. It began to climb the charts and by January 1956 it had reached the top ten. The craze took off and thousands of teenagers quickly formed skiffle bands, including The Quarrymen with John Lennon, Paul McCartney and George Harrison. Following the success of 'Rock Island Line', Donegan fell out with Chris Barber and called himself the 'King of Skiffle'. He had a few more hits such as 'Cumberland Gap', the comedy 'Does your chewing gum lose its flavour on the bedpost overnight', and 'My old man's a dustman'. He died in 2002.

Ronnie Scott, Tubby Hayes

Both Ronnie Scott and Tubby Hayes recorded numerous times at Decca. On 31 July 1956 the album entitled *Jazz at the Flamingo* was recorded at the Railway Hotel next door pretending to be the Flamingo! The band consisted of Ronnie Scott (tenor sax), Tubby Hayes (tenor sax), Harry Klein (baritone sax), Terry Shannon (piano), Lennie Bush (bass) and Tony Crombie (drums). Jazz journalist Alun Morgan heard on the news that Jim Laker had famously taken all ten wickets in the test match at Old Trafford against Australia. When he told Tony Crombie, who was not a cricket buff, Crombie said, 'Is that good?' Eventually impressed, he decided to call one of the tunes 'Laker's Day'. What the musicians probably did not know, was that Jim Laker lived just half a mile down the road from the Decca Studios at No. 30a Priory Terrace.

Larry Parnes and his boys

From the late 1950s and into the '60s Larry Parnes managed numerous pop stars, many of whom, including Tommy Steele, Billy Fury, Joe Brown, and Georgie Fame, recorded at Decca Studios. A flamboyant gay man, Parnes, who was nicknamed 'Parnes, shillings and pence' because he paid his stars so little, signed handsome male singers and gave them evocative pseudonyms. Joe Brown was the only one who resisted Parnes' renaming. One can see why, when he was told he was going to be named 'Elmer Twitch'. In 1958 Parnes began his concept of the package tour, when his stable of stars toured in a bus playing in a punishing schedule of one night stands around the country. Parnes auditioned and turned down the Silver Beetles (as The Beatles were previously known) as a backing band for Billy Fury. But he did employ them to back Johnny Gentle in 1960. In 1967 he retired from the pop music world and went into theatre management. He died in August 1989.

POPULAR MUSIC FROM THE 1960s

The Beatles

On New Year's Day 1962, The Beatles auditioned at Decca Studios. Their manager Brian Epstein, who ran a chain of record shops in Liverpool, had written about the group to 'Disker', a reviewer for the *Liverpool Echo*. He was rather surprised when he got an answer from Tony Barrow in London. Barrow was 'Disker' and he had begun writing the column 'Off The Record' for the paper when he was still at school in Crosby but he was now working for Decca, writing sleeve notes on the back of LPs. Epstein phoned Barrow and they arranged to meet in London. Tony Barrow said:

> When he came down and saw me at Decca, Brian brought me an acetate which was The Beatles at the Cavern Club. It was absolutely appalling. I mean, in terms of capturing the excitement of their Cavern Club sound, maybe it was okay, but in terms of showing what The Beatles were like, it was appalling. I kind of said so. I didn't do a 'don't call us, we'll call you', because it wasn't my place to do so.
>
> I was strictly a sleeve note writer and had nothing to do with A&R (Artists and Repertoire), or with signing the acts ... After Brian left, I made a call on the internal phone, not to the A&R department, but to the marketing people, because I was aware that Brian Epstein was a record retailer who had a record shop and maybe, just maybe, the sales people at Decca would be interested in giving one of their customers an audition.

(David Pritchard and Alan Lysaght,
The Beatles: An Oral History, 1998)

As a result of this, Epstein had a meeting with the marketing people at Decca, who told Dick Rowe, the A&R manager, about The Beatles. Rowe had a team consisting of his assistant Mike Smith, sound engineer Peter Attwood and Tony Meehan. Tony had been The Shadows' first drummer. He left The Shadows in September 1961 and joined Decca as a producer. Looking for new talent, Dick Rowe sent Mike Smith to Liverpool to see The Beatles. Smith and Epstein

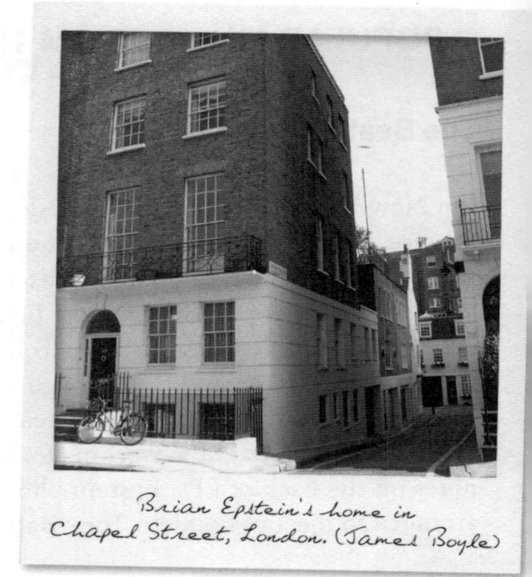

Brian Epstein's home in Chapel Street, London. (James Boyle)

The Beatles with drummer Pete Best

(With kind permission of Joe Flannery, from his book Standing in the Wings: The Beatles, Brian Epstein and Me)

went to see the group at the Cavern on 13 December 1961. Smith was impressed and an audition was arranged in London for 1 January 1962.

Back in 1962, New Year's Day wasn't a holiday but Dick Rowe was away, and it was left to Mike Smith to organise the session. Brian Epstein travelled to London by train but John Lennon, Paul McCartney, George Harrison and drummer Pete Best had to drive down the previous day with their equipment. The freezing weather, with fog and snow, meant the journey took ten hours. After getting lost, The Beatles finally arrived at the Royal Hotel in Woburn Place around 10 p.m. on New Year's Eve. Pete Best, who was replaced by Ringo Starr on 16 August 1962, recalled what happened:

> Brian Epstein had read the riot act to us before we went down to London. You know, be good little boys, you mustn't be out after 10 o'clock. And there we were with everyone else in the middle of Trafalgar Square as drunk as skunks. We were late getting to Decca Studios the next day. Brian was there before us. He was livid and tore a strip off us left, right and centre. John said, Brian shut up, we are here for the audition.

(TV documentary, *Love Me Do; The Beatles '62*, 2012)

They arrived at the studios in Broadhurst Gardens by 11 a.m., but Mike Smith was over an hour late, having been held up by the snow. The Beatles briefly met Tony Meehan, who went into the producer's box, and they started to set up their equipment. However, the Decca technicians and Mike Smith asked them to use the equipment in the studio.

Over the next three hours The Beatles played fifteen songs, which were mainly cover versions; only three were Lennon and McCartney originals ('Like Dreamers Do', 'Hello Little Girl' and 'Love Of The Loved'). Epstein had persuaded them to do a set which he thought would show their range of ability, including 'Besame Mucho', 'The Sheik Of Araby', 'Money', and 'Till There Was You'. Clearly the group weren't at their best after the long journey and a night of heavy drinking; Lennon and McCartney later said they'd wanted to do more rock numbers.

Weeks went by after the audition and Epstein was frustrated at not getting an answer from Decca, so he contacted a number of other companies, including Columbia, Oriole, Philips and Pye. All of them turned The Beatles down, based on what they heard from the Decca session.

Brian Poole and the Tremelos auditioned at Decca later that same afternoon. Mike Smith wanted to sign both groups but Dick Rowe said they could only take one and told Smith to choose. He went with the Tremelos because their audition was better than The Beatles', and he thought it would be easier to work with a Dagenham band than a Liverpool-based group. After numerous phone calls, Epstein was invited to lunch with Dick Rowe and the head of marketing on 6 February. He was told that Decca had decided not to sign The Beatles. In his autobiography Epstein said he couldn't believe his ears:

> You must be out of your tiny little minds! These boys are going to explode. I am completely confident that one day they will be bigger than Elvis Presley!

He also said that Rowe told him:

> Not to mince words, Mr Epstein, we don't like your boys' sound. Groups of guitars are on the way out ... Your boys are never going to get off the ground. We know what we're talking about. You really should stick to selling recordings in Liverpool.

(Brian Epstein, *A Cellarful of Noise*, London: Souvenir, 1964)

Rowe denies that he said this, and maintained Epstein made it up because he was so annoyed at being rejected. But the story stuck and although Mike Smith initially made the decision, Rowe has gone down in history as 'the man who turned down the Beatles'. But this is unfair. As Andrew Oldham, the manager of The Rolling Stones, points out in his autobiography, *Stoned*, everybody who heard their Decca session turned them down.

It is now possible to hear the Decca session for yourself on YouTube. Most critics agree that it's hard to appreciate The Beatles' potential from this material. The Beatles didn't perform well nor did their unique talent emerge, particularly as there were only three original songs.

As most people know, The Beatles were signed by EMI Parlophone. Epstein met George Martin, the EMI producer, on 13 February. Martin says he noted the confidence that Epstein had in The Beatles. Although he was not particularly impressed when he heard the Decca sessions demo, Martin was struck by a freshness in the three titles composed by John Lennon and Paul McCartney. In May, George Martin told Epstein that he intended to sign The Beatles. On 6 June they did a test recording at Abbey Road which included three Lennon and McCartney songs, 'Love Me Do', 'Ask Me Why', and 'P.S. I Love You', as well as the standard 'Besame Mucho'. They were signed to Parlophone, with the contract backdated to 4 June so that EMI kept ownership of the 6 June session. The Beatles first proper recording was done at Abbey Road on 4 September. Their first single, 'Love Me Do', was released on 5 October 1962 and went into the charts the following week.

Alexis Korner and Cyril Davies, 'Blues Incorporated'

On 17 March 1962 guitarist Alexis Korner and singer and harmonica player Cyril Davies set up their own club in a basement below the ABC Tea Shop in Ealing, to play R&B.

This soon attracted like-minded people who were interested in the blues. TV producer Jack Good persuaded a reluctant Decca to record the band at the West Hampstead studios on 8 June 1962. Because the Decca officials didn't believe that the Blues would take off, it was released in November 1962 on a budget label as 'R&B from the Marquee'. They were very surprised when it sold in thousands and continues to do so today.

The Rolling Stones

Having not signed The Beatles, Decca were fortunate that they did manage to get The Rolling Stones. Dick Rowe had been tipped off by George Harrison that The Rolling Stones were playing at the Station Hotel in Richmond and he went to see them. On 11 March 1963 the Stones went to IBC studios in Portland Place to record five tracks, 'Roadrunner', 'Bright Lights Big City', 'Diddley Diddley Daddy', 'Honey, What's Wrong', and 'I Wanna Be Loved', with producer Glyn Johns. The tapes failed to make an impression on any of the record labels approached. So they recut Chuck Berry's 'Come On' and Willie Dixon's 'I Wanna Be Loved' at Olympic Studios on 10 May 1963. With a strong push from Decca's Dick Rowe, they went to the West Hampstead studios to do yet another recording of the tracks

Mick Jagger and The Rolling Stones still selling out stadiums in 2007 (here) and today. (Gonzalo Andrés)

with producer Mike Barclay. Dick Rowe then signed them to Decca and the Stones' debut single was released on 7 June. It reached Number 20 in the British charts.

On 9 July 1963 the Stones recorded two tracks, 'Poison Ivy' and 'Fortune Teller', at Decca Studios, with producer Michael Barclay and engineer Gus Dudgeon. These were scheduled for release as a single on 26 August 1963, but withdrawn. They were later released on a compilation record on 25 January 1964.

Songs 'Bye Bye Johnny' and 'You Better Move On' were recorded on 8 August 1963, with Andrew Loog Oldham as the producer. The tracks appeared on *The Rolling Stones* (EP) on 10 January 1964. Although released on the Decca label, most of the subsequent Stones recordings were not done at West Hampstead but at a number of other London studios, such as Regent Sound and de Lane Lea.

Lulu

The 14-year-old Marie Lawrie was discovered in Glasgow by Tony Gordon, who was opening a nightclub there. In 1963 she came to London with her band and first met Ron Richards of EMI at an un-named studio in West Hampstead. After the audition, Richards said they weren't right for EMI but suggested that they went to see Peter Sullivan at Decca Studios, so they drove round the corner to Broadhurst Gardens. The technicians had to call a temporary halt while recording the Isley Brothers' 'Shout', as Marie's powerful voice had broken the delicate ribbon element in her microphone. She also recorded Gene Pitney's '24 Hours from Tulsa'. Tony Gordon and his sister Marian Massey thought Marie was a 'real lulu of a kid' and decided to rebrand her as 'Lulu'. Marian Massey became her long-time manager and mentor. Decca released 'Shout' as a single on 15 April 1964 and it quickly became a huge success. In 1969 Lulu lived with husband Maurice Gibb from the BeeGees, in Priory Terrace, West Hampstead, before moving to Compton Avenue near Highgate, where Ringo Starr also lived.

David Bowie (David Jones)

David Bowie was born as David Jones and he went through a number of name changes and different bands. Bromley school friends George Underwood and David Jones joined The Konrads who had formed in 1962. On 30 August 1963 The Konrads, with David Jones (vocals), Roger Ferris (vocals), George Underwood (guitar and vocals), Neville Wills (guitar), Alan Dodds (guitar) and Dave Crook (drums), went to Decca Studios for the first time and recorded 'I Never Dreamed'. Soon after this recording, David and George left the band, though the band stayed together playing the club circuit, and they toured as the opening act with The Rolling Stones.

David Bowie's first single release 'Liza Jane', credited to Davie Jones with The King Bees, was released on 5 June 1964 on Decca's Vocalion Pop label. It was backed with 'Louie Louie Go Home', which was initially pencilled in as the A-side. The King Bees was formed in November 1963 by David and George. The band members were Davie Jones (vocals), George Underwood (harmonica and guitar), Roger Fluck (guitar), Dave Howard (bass)

David Bowie performing in 1990. (Jorge Barrios)

and Robert Allen (drums). George remembered feeling quite nervous while recording at Decca and it wasn't helped when producer Glyn Johns said his guitar wasn't tuned properly.

The original 'Liza Jane' single is now highly collectable. Leslie Conn, a music agent who managed The King Bees, talking in 1997 said:

> When David and I parted company I went off to live and work in Majorca for a few years and one day I was on the phone to my mother and she said, 'What shall I do with those records I have in the garage' which were a few hundred copies of 'Liza Jane'. So I replied, 'Throw them out', and she did. The last time David came up here he said, 'Have you got any of those records we made, you know they're worth over a hundred pounds each!' I told him I got my mother to throw them all out! We had to laugh.
>
> (www.bowiewonderworld.com)

David Bowie became a major Decca artist, but most of the subsequent recordings were done at independent studios, not at Broadhurst Gardens.

Having attended Beckenham Art School, George Underwood produced distinctive album covers for T.Rex, Gentle Giant and David Bowie's *Hunky Dory* and *Ziggy Stardust*. After recording a single under the name of Calvin James, for Mickie Most, he left the music business to concentrate on art.

An interesting connection to Klooks Kleek is that Dick Jordan, who set up the club (*see* Chapter Three), later worked for Folio, who represented George Underwood. Folio, a major company which is still going today, was set up by Nick Dawe in 1976 as an agency for artists.

The Zombies

The Zombies, from St Albans, formed in 1961 and consisted of Colin Blunstone (vocals), Rod Argent (keyboards), Chris White (bass), Paul Atkinson (guitar) and Hugh Grundy (drums).

In 1964, The Zombies had their first session at Broadhurst Gardens and recorded 'It's Alright With Me', 'She's Not There', 'Summertime' and 'You Make Me Feel Good'. Their single 'She's Not There' was released on 24 July 1964 and became a hit record for the group. Their other big hit was 'Time Of The Season' (1968). The band also achieved considerable success in America.

Colin Blunstone recalled what happened at Decca:

> We recorded in the evening. So, we went in about seven and I think we were probably finished by ten, something like that and it was done. They recorded very, very fast in those days. I must tell you just one story. We got that session and we had a fine producer and engineer, but because it was in the evening, at lunch time, the engineer had been at a wedding. And he got very drunk. He also became very aggressive. We never met him before. I remember thinking if this is the recording industry, I don't think this is for me. That was my first session. But we were quite lucky 'cause he passed out. And so four of us got an arm or leg and we had to carry him up a flight of stairs and put him in the back of a black London taxi. And off he went home. His assistant took over and his assistant was Gus Dudgeon and that was Gus Dudgeon's first session and our first session. And of course he went on to produce Elton John, David Bowie, Kiki Dee and many others. I worked with Gus subsequently and sadly he's no longer with us. He always remembered that first session, and so did we. It was quite a fiery introduction to recording studios.

(www.classicbands.com)

The Zombies did their next recording at Decca Studios, with producer Ken Jones, on 31 August 1964. The A-side of the single was 'Leave Me Be'. In 1965, The Zombies recorded 'She's Coming Home', 'Remember You', 'Just Out of Reach', 'I Want You Back Again', 'I Must Move', 'Come on Time' and a 'Bunny Lake is Missing' promo at Decca Studios.

Van Morrison and Them

On 5 July 1964, Van Morrison, aged only 18, and the other members of the band Them were recorded by Dick Rowe at Decca Studios. Rowe had travelled to Belfast to see the group and signed them for a two-year Decca deal. 'Turn on Your Love Light' and their biggest hit 'Gloria' were recorded during this session, as were both sides of their first single. The band took their name from a 1954 sci-fi horror film. In addition to Van Morrison on vocals, harmonica and sax, the band members were Alan Henderson (bass), Billy Harrison (guitar), Ronny Millings (drums) and Pat McAuley (keys). Their first singles, 'Don't Start Crying Now' and 'One Two Brown Eyes' were released in August, but did not prove successful. Their next singles 'Baby Please Don't Go' and 'Gloria' were released in November. In December 1964 they made their TV debut on *Ready Steady Go*, along with The Rolling Stones. Their manager, Phil Solomon, got 'Gloria' used as the show's signature tune and within two weeks it had entered the Hit Parade. Van Morrison left the band in 1966 and went on to a very successful career as a solo artist.

Marc Bolan

Marc Bolan was born Mark Feld in Hackney on 30 September 1947. He was best known as the lead singer with the glam rock band T.Rex:

> On the morning of 14 September 1965, Mike Leander, Jim Economides, Mike Pruskin, and Marc Bolan were at Decca

Studios in West Hampstead. A small backing orchestra, comprising string sections and pop instruments, and The Ladybirds vocal group were briefed and awaiting further instructions from Leander. It was ten in the morning and everyone knew the session would be over by lunchtime. Three songs were recorded that morning: two originals, 'The Wizard' and 'Beyond The Risin' Sun'; and a Chicago blues song, 'That's The Bag I'm In'. The first two were coupled for Marc Bolan's debut single, 'The Wizard' which was released on 19 November 1965.

(Mark Paytress, *Bolan: The Rise and Fall of a 20th Century Superstar,* Omnibus Press, 2002)

In 1965, George Melly, the singer and critic, wrote a piece in *The Observer.* He had been invited by Mike Pruskin to Decca Studios to hear this first recording by Marc Bolan. Mike Pruskin, a cousin of Lionel Bart, would ring George Melly up regularly to enthuse about a new band. Melly wrote:

Bolan comes from a family of Soho costermongers. He has modelled, acted, bummed around France and Italy. He is only 17 now and looks much younger. He's quiet and shy. At the studio there was a large group of musicians, including a flautist, a small choir of ladies to make oooo noises, the arranger, who also conducted, and an American A&R man to supervise the whole session. Bolan recorded a song he had written about a wizard ... The A&R man, Mr Economides, with many chart successes to his name, insisted on a great many takes ... He wore a tennis sweater, and was as cool and detached as a surgeon. However, he finally declared himself 'gassed'.

(*The Observer*, 26 September 1965)

Other tracks – 'Highways', 'Rings of Fortune', 'Reality' and 'Song for a Soldier' – were recorded at Decca in December 1965. The producer was again Jim Economides and the music director was Mike Leander. Mike Pruskin was Bolan's publicist and manager. Later recordings were made at de Lane Lea studios in Kingsway and other independent studios.

Bolan died on 16 September 1977, two weeks before his 30th birthday. He never learned to drive and was the passenger in a car which hit a metal fence and tree in Barnes, south-west London. The driver was his American girlfriend and singer, Gloria Jones. She survived the crash, after suffering a broken arm and jaw. They were driving home to East Sheen from a restaurant in Berkeley Square.

Tom Jones

In 1964, Decca producer Peter Sullivan saw Tom Woodward when he was the singer with Tommy Scott and the Senators' who played the clubs in South Wales. Sullivan was impressed with Tom Woodward and soon Gordon Mills became his manager. Mills called him Tom Jones after the film of the same name. 'It's Not Unusual', written by Les Reed and Gordon Scott, became Tom Jones' first big hit, and was recorded at Decca Studios

Tom Jones, still extremely popular today, here performing at Hampton Court Palace in 2007. (Georgio)

on 14 December 1964. The song was originally planned for Sandie Shaw, but when she heard Tom's demo, she said that he should record it. The record was produced by Peter Sullivan and the backing band consisted of some of the leading British musicians, including Kenny Baker (trumpet), Ronnie Ross (sax), Joe Moretti (guitar), Vic Flick (guitar) and Andy White (drums).

Tom Jones became very popular in America, where he currently lives, and has continued singing over a long and successful career. In 2012 and 2013 he was a judge on the BBC TV talent programme *The Voice*.

Moody Blues

The group were formed in Birmingham in 1964. Originally an R&B band, which played at Klooks Kleek, they changed their style. They had called themselves the 'MB Five' hoping to get sponsorship from the Mitchell and Butler brewery, but when this didn't materialise, they were renamed as The Moody Blues and signed to Decca. In December 1964 their second single 'Go Now' was a Number 1 hit in the UK; it also reached Number 10 in the US the following year.

When Denny Lane and Clint Warwick left the band they were replaced by John Lodge and Justin Hayward in November 1966. In October 1967 the group also included Mike Pinder, Graeme Edge and Ray Thomas. The album *Days of Future Passed* was recorded at Decca's Studio One between 8 October and 3 November 1967, with producer Tony Clarke and engineer Derek Varnals, who created a symphonic sound. A track from the album, 'Nights in White Satin', released on 10 November, became a huge hit for the band in England and in the US the following April. The band continued to work in Broadhurst Gardens with Tony Clarke and Derek Varnals. In 1974 they took over Studio One as their own Threshold Studios until Decca Studios closed in 1981.

The Moody Blues have been very successful, selling more than 70 million albums worldwide and have been awarded a total of fourteen platinum and gold discs.

Champion Jack Dupree

Dupree was originally from Chicago but after touring in England a number of times, he settled in Halifax. In February 1966, 'New Orleans To Chicago' was recorded at Decca Studios with Eric Clapton and featuring John Mayall on some tracks. The producer was Mike Vernon.

John Mayall's Bluesbreakers

John Mayall was very good at spotting new musicians for his band and several key albums were recorded at Decca Studios. The first was *Mayall Plays Mayall* recorded at Klooks Kleek on 7 December 1964, when cables were run over to the next-door studios. The band at this time was Mayall (vocals, keyboards and harmonica), Roger Dean (guitar), John McVie (bass), Hughie Flint (drums) and Nigel Stanger (sax).

Probably their most famous album, *Bluesbreakers: John Mayall with Eric Clapton*, was recorded in March 1966. The band was Mayall (keyboards and vocals), Clapton (guitar), John McVie (bass), and Hughie Flint (drums). A horn section was added later. The *Beano Album*, as it was called because Clapton is seen reading the comic on the cover, was released on 22 July 1966. But Clapton left soon after to form Cream with Jack Bruce and Ginger Baker. Mayall persuaded guitarist Peter Green to come back and replace Clapton, and a series of recordings were made at Decca Studios in September and October 1966. The album, called *A Hard Road*, was released in February 1967. In June, Green left to form Peter Green's Fleetwood Mac with Mick Fleetwood and John McVie. At this point Mayall hired 18-year-old guitarist Mick Taylor and in July 1967 they recorded the album *Crusade* with the new line-up.

In April 1968, with producer Mike Vernon and engineer Derek Varnals, Mayall recorded the *Bare Wires* album. This included a twenty-three-minute version of the song 'Bare Wires Suite' with a jazzier feel. Listening carefully, one of the songs, 'Fire', has a backing track of people making love played backwards. Later that year, Mayall recorded *Blues from Laurel Canyon* on 26–28 August 1968 at Decca Studios, with the same producer and engineer.

Mayall had a reputation as a difficult band leader, but people who worked with him said he was very fair. When Keef Hartley was asked what it was like to work with Mayall, he jokingly said, 'John made us get up at six o'clock in the morning and run round Hyde Park,' which wasn't true. John didn't allow the band to take drugs or be drunk, however, and various band members developed techniques to hide their 'habits' from him.

Peter Green's Fleetwood Mac

The original line-up of Fleetwood Mac was Peter Green, Mick Fleetwood and John McVie. Recording after hours at Decca Studios, with Mike Vernon in June and July 1967, the first album they produced was simply called *Fleetwood Mac*. Later, Green asked guitarist Jeremy Spencer to join them. Mike Vernon had supported and signed the band to his new label, Blue Horizon.

Ten Years After

The band which began in the Mansfield and Nottingham area as the Jaybirds, changed their name to Ten Years After in 1966, when they moved to London. The name is a reference to Elvis Presley's hugely successful year, 1956. After several personnel changes, the band consisted of Alvin Lee (vocal and guitar), Ric Lee (no relation, drums), Leo Lyons (bass), and Chick Churchill (keys). The group signed to Decca in 1967. Their first album was not a big commercial success, but the second album *Undead*, recorded at Klooks Kleek in 1968, and which contained 'I'm Going Home', a six-minute blues featuring Alvin's guitar solo, hit the charts on both sides of the Atlantic.

Ric Lee wrote about making *Undead* at Klooks:

> Our first release, 'Ten Years After', despite receiving critical acclaim and being greatly appreciated by our fans had failed, in our estimation, to capture the excitement of our live performances. 'Undead' came about for several reasons: First, to capture on record the raw energy of the band and to display what Mike Vernon, our producer, said on the original sleeve notes were 'musical gymnastics coupled with inventiveness, that was most exciting on stage in front of an appreciative audience'. Secondly, Bill Graham, promoter at the Fillmore Ballroom in San Francisco, USA, impressed with our first album, had invited us to play his venue, 'should we be in the States at anytime'. Fired up by this invite, we did everything we could to get ourselves to the US. We had begun recording what was to be 'Stonedhenge', our third album, but it was a more experimental album and completion by June, when our first American tour was scheduled, would have been impossible. The obvious thing was to record a 'live' album. Originally, 'Undead' was intended for US release only, to go with our first tour there, but Deram relented and released it later in the UK following highly vociferous protests by our fans.
>
> On Tuesday May 14th 1968, we played to a packed house at Klook's Kleek, a jazz era name for a funky, upstairs room, at the Railway Hotel, West Hampstead, North London. Run by Dick Jordan, this sweaty, dusty club played host to bands on the mushrooming blues circuit; John Mayall, Fleetwood Mac, Chicken Shack and many others. Klook's was practically next door to Decca studios and John Mayall

had already recorded from there by tossing mic leads over the roof into Studio Two's mixing desk. Unfortunately, when we wanted to record 'Undead', Studio Two was booked for another session and we were unable to use what had become our 'home'. Roy Baker, later to become Roy Thomas Baker, producer of Queen, and tape operator Peter Rynston, solved the problem by dragging a mixing desk used for classical location sessions into the canteen at the back of Decca studios' complex. They fitted limiters, echo and reverb, doctored the wiring and again threw leads across the roof to Klook's. I remember setting up my drum kit at the back of the postage stamp stage, no risers or monitors for drums in that period.

(Sleeve notes on TYA album *Undead*)

TYA's big breakthrough came from their appearance at the 1969 Woodstock Festival, where they stunned the audience with a nine-minute version of 'I'm Going Home'. They played at the Isle of Wight Festival in 1970 and were in great demand; by 1974 they had made twenty-eight US tours, which was a record for any British band. Alvin Lee left the band and went solo. He died in Spain, where he had been living for some time, on 6 March 2013. The rest of TYA continue to tour today.

Ric Lee, 2009.
(Axel Hindemith)

Keef Hartley

Drummer Keef's friendship with producer Mike Vernon enabled him to play on many great albums. Joining friends such as Eric Clapton, Tony McPhee, Peter Green, Mick Taylor and John Mayall, he played on countless sessions for visiting American bluesmen, such as Champion Jack Dupree and Jimmy Witherspoon. This informal group of friends also worked on many other LP's that Mike Vernon produced for Decca and later Blue Horizon. As Keef explains:

> Mike had the job of preparing many American blues albums for their British release. Unfortunately many were already recorded in mono, but the market demanded stereo records by the mid to late sixties. So we were given the job of learning the tracks note for note, including all the bum ones, which Mike would then mix with the original master to create a new stereo version. It was strange to do, but extremely well paid so nobody seemed to mind.

Keef was keen to move on and he began auditioning for a new band. The nucleus of this was Peter (Dino) Dines (keyboards), Spit James, better known as Ian Cruickshank (guitar), Gary Thain (bass), Keef (drums) and Owen Finnegan (vocals). The Keef Hartley Band began to work regularly and their Chicago-based blues rock was getting a good audience response. Keef took the band into Decca Studios to record their first album, produced by Neil Slavin, but listening to the tracks it was evident that Owen's vocals didn't sound right on the recording. Auditions for a new singer brought Miller Anderson to the fore and they returned to the studio and re-recorded the vocals. The *Halfbreed* album was issued in 1969 by Deram, housed in a striking gatefold sleeve. This showed Keef dressed in full Red Indian costume, which reflected his admiration for native American culture.

John Mayall was known for both hiring and firing people in his band at short notice. At the beginning of the album, as a joke, John Mayall and Keef recreate the moment when John fired Keef. Trumpet player Henry Lowther said he went to hear Mayall playing one weekend and John said, 'Do you want a job?' The following Monday, Henry was in the van with the rest of the band travelling to Southampton to play a gig. Henry said, 'There were never rehearsals, we just got there and played.' Henry also played with the Keef Hartley Band.

The *Halfbreed* album was well received and entered the British and American charts. A US tour was quickly arranged and the band followed Santana on stage at the August 1969 Woodstock Festival. However, their performance doesn't appear in the subsequent highly successful film of the festival because their manager wanted a written contract from Martin Scorsese before he would give permission.

The second album, recorded at Decca Studios in 1969, is called *The Battle of North West Six* because of the problems over volume levels Keef had with Derek Varnals, the recording engineer. Both Keef and Derek later told Dick Weindling it was a difficult session. Sadly, Keef died on 26 November 2011 in Preston.

Henry Lowther

Trumpet player and multi-instrumentalist Henry Lowther, worked as a session man on hundreds of recordings for Decca. In 2013 he told Dick Weindling that when his own album *Child Song* was made in 1970, Neil Slavin was the producer and Derek Varnals was the engineer. He remembered there was a track with five trumpets and four violins overdubbed. As part of a percussion link between two tracks, Henry wanted a big gong sound but they didn't have one in the studio. The problem was solved by using a recording with a gong sound and cutting the tape with a razor and splicing it in.

Bing Crosby

It is little known that Bing recorded at Decca Studios. The year before he died he made the 12 track album called *Feels Good, Feels Right*, on 20–22 July and 17 August 1976 with the Alan Cohen jazz orchestra. The producer was Kevin Daly and the engineer was Martin Smith. Henry Lowther, who played trumpet on the session, said he was very impressed with Bing's professionalism. Henry remembered how Bing wanted to be with the musicians as they played rather than be separated from them in a booth, which the engineers preferred for the recording.

The Specials

In early May 1979, The Specials played at the Moonlight Club in the Railway Hotel, to a packed house of fans and record company executives. Even Mick Jagger was there, anxious to sign the band to his own Rolling Stone Records. The session was captured through an audio feed to Decca Studios next door. The bootleg features plenty of singer Terry Hall's dry humour on the eve of the Thatcher election, along with a great live performance. The bootleg made it onto the streets just days before their debut album, *Specials*, was released on Two Tone Records in October 1979. Marianne Colloms was a guest at Terry's wedding reception and has a CD of the invite, which was a specially recorded song.

The Moonlight Tapes

One of the last recordings made at Decca Studios consisted of live performances by various bands at the Moonlight Club in the Railway Hotel next door, from 27 April to 2 May 1980.

DECCA RECORD PRODUCERS AND ENGINEERS

Arthur Haddy, Recording Engineer

As described earlier, Haddy was the main engineer for Crystalate and later played a vital role in the development of recording technology for Decca. He was awarded an OBE in 1976 for his work in recording and for his wartime contribution.

Arthur Lilley, Recording Engineer

Like Haddy, Arther Lilley was an early engineer at Decca, which he joined in 1932. He was born in Wandsworth, the eldest of five children. His father ran a hairdressing business in Westminster and many of the Members of Parliament were his clients. Arthur's mother was a dancer and she may have met her husband at the Drury Lane Theatre where Lilley senior was a part-time saxophone player. Arthur had no formal training in music, but he played piano and double bass. Arthur used to go to Decca Studios at Broadhurst Gardens in his lunch break to play the piano. He started to work there as an office boy/receptionist and eventually became an engineer. Lilley was very artistic and used to draw caricatures of the stars as they came into the studios.

After the war, Arthur resumed his career at Decca Studios and soon became a recording engineer of note, particularly for Mantovani and his orchestra. He also recorded with the leading popular stars of the time, including Winifred Atwell, Mrs Mills and Russ Conway, bandleader Billy Cotton, vocal group The Beverley Sisters, and singers Vera Lynn, Billy Fury, Anthony Newley, Joan Regan, Lita Roza, Max Bygraves, Jimmy Young, David Whitfield and many others. He was a very adaptive engineer. His daughter Susan remembers that Tommy Steele could not whistle a certain note on his hit 'Singing The Blues', so after many attempts Arthur cut it out and filled it in later. With Winnie Atwell he took the back off her piano to create a honky tonk effect on her single 'Black And White Rag' which later became the signature tune of the TV programme *Pot Black*.

Lilley would turn up for a Mantovani recording three hours before anyone else. If there had been a rock session the night before, Arthur would patiently re-jig everything in the studio. Rock musicians needed felt carpets to produce a tight sound, but Mantovani's requirements were exactly the opposite, so the carpets were removed to get a reverberant sound which gave a degree of echo to reinforce the strings. Arthur would then set up the studio almost as he would for a symphony orchestra, putting as many as nine microphones on the strings and seven on the other instruments. Monty (as he was called) would usually arrive half an hour before the rest of the musicians and while he was rehearsing them Arthur would balance the sound controls. Monty would tell Arthur what he wanted, but didn't interfere with sound technicalities; he had complete trust in Arthur's professionalism. The two men were both painstakingly creative perfectionists. In the 1950s a local paper commented about the studios:

> Strains of the unique sound of Mantovani's orchestra, of the Show Band, of the famous voices of Vera Lynn, Lita Rosa, Joan Regan and Dickie Valentine float over the rooftops, all day and everyday.

Hugh Mendl, Producer

Hugh Mendl (1919–2008) worked for Decca as a record producer and A&R executive for over four decades. Graduating from Oxford University College, Mendl planned to undertake a career in government; however, his love of jazz music caused him to reconsider. A family connection to Decca (his grandfather was chairman) helped him to obtain a position as a post boy from where he worked his way up. The outbreak of the Second World War meant that Mendl was sent to Jerusalem, where he became an announcer for a local jazz radio station. Returning to Decca when peacetime came Mendl became the company's first 'radio plugger' and worked to promote the label and their artists. In 1950, Mendl turned producer and was soon working with Winifred Atwell (recording the classic 'Black and White Rag').

A great fan of American jazz musicians, such as Louis Armstrong and Duke Ellington, Mendl went to the 100 Club in Oxford Street where a new, young British jazz scene was emerging. Mendl got the Chris Barber band into the studio in July 1954 and recorded an album called *New Orleans Joys*. This included Lonnie Donegan playing 'Rock Island Line'. When it was released as a single it started the skiffle craze.

Mendl next signed Tommy Steele, who he discovered at the 2i's coffee bar in Soho, stealing a march on George Martin from EMI, who also went to the same venue and signed the less successful skiffle act, Wally Whyton and the Vipers. Mendl had booked Tommy Steele for an audition at Decca Studios but due to a mix up, no studios were free, so he had to hear him with just a bass and drums in the artists' rest room. He sang 'Rock with the Cavemen'. Mendl said, 'Everyone was being rude about rock 'n' roll but this was such a magical performance and he had such a dynamic personality that, after only a chorus or two, I stopped him and said, "Yes, this is absolutely perfect."' A few days later, on 24 September 1956, he went into the studios and recorded 'Rock with Cavemen' and 'Rock Around The Town'. 'Cavemen' had been co-written at an all-night party by Tommy Steele, Lionel Bart and Mike Pratt, and was based on the story of the Piltdown Man hoax.

Mendl was the executive producer for The Moody Blues and their 1967 album *Days of Future Passed.* Under his guidance they would receive acclaim as a popular rock group. Mendl was also able to introduce the concept of an orchestral album with The Moody Blues, a deal which would effectively reveal the abilities of Decca Studios impressive stereo technique. Mendl also signed a number of prominent artists, including John Mayall and the Bluesbreakers, David Bowie, Caravan and Genesis. In addition he produced the original recordings of a number of musicals including *Oh! What a Lovely War,* and *Helly, Dolly!* among others.

Soon after Mendl suffered a stroke in late 1979 the Decca company was taken over by Polygram and as such he never returned to work there. He left the music industry and moved to Devon where he ran an antiques shop.

Tony D'Amato, Producer

In 1958, New York-born Tony D'Amato joined London Records, the US arm of Decca. In 1961 he came to work in the Broadhurst Gardens studios and was at first regarded with some suspicion. But his work with Mantovani helped sell huge numbers of records and he became part of the team. Much of his bond with Mantovani came from their shared Italian origins. He would poke fun at himself, saying that he had two main moods at Decca, a tranquil one around Mantovani and a confrontational one at their main offices, Decca House, on the embankment. He also produced records for bandleaders Ted Heath and Edmundo Ros.

Mike Vernon, Producer

Mike Vernon is renowned amongst blues fans for his work during the British blues boom of the late 1960s, when he worked as a prominent producer. He joined Decca in 1962, describing his early position as that of a 'gofer – make the tea, go for this, go for that'. However, he went on to work with popular artists including Fleetwood Mac, Chick Shack, Peter Green and Ten Years After, among many others. A number of these would be released on his legendary Blue Horizon label which he co-created alongside his brother Richard Vernon and Neil Slavin in 1966. Vernon also worked with Eric Clapton on the cutting-edge Bluesbreaking album after meeting John Mayall. In fact, he is known to have told Hugh Mendl, 'We need to pay some attention to John Mayall's Bluesbreakers, especially now he's got this young ex-Yardbird guitar player, Eric Clapton, who's turning the blues scene completely upside down.'

Mendl told him to get them signed up to Decca and this led to the well-known Bluesbreakers' *Beano* album. It was recorded Decca Studios over four days in March 1966 and it proved difficult to persuade the Decca engineers to allow Clapton to play so loud. Luckily, the young engineer Gus Dudgeon saw this as a challenge. He moved the mics between four and six feet away from Clapton's Marshall amps, rather than placing them just in front, but the high sound levels were still a problem:

> Gus could hear guitar leaking onto everything, it was so loud. Mike and Gus reasoned that the only way to solve this was to do a take, and then gauge Eric's response to a playback. They recorded the first title, called the guys into the control room, and rolled the tape. Gus says; 'Eric loved it and he grinned from ear to ear. He took on the rules and broke them.'

(Mo Foster, *17 Watts? The Birth of British Rock Guitar*, 1997)

Vernon also produced the first demos of the band that would become Fleetwood Mac, and he was allowed to use the studios on Sundays mornings to audition new bands. In February 1968 he left Decca, but three weeks later signed a contract with them as an independent producer and went on to produce a huge number of records by many of the best blues bands.

Gus Dudgeon, Engineer and Producer

When Gus Dudgeon left school he got a job as the tea boy at Olympic Studios near Baker Street. He was 'blown away' by the power of the studio speakers with their tremendous bass and treble ranges. Desperate to play with the controls, he said, 'I was terrified at the idea of ever getting onto the recording console.' He managed to get a job as an engineer at Decca Studios in 1962. During his five and a half years there, Dudgeon engineered The Zombies' hit 'She's Not There' (1964) and, as described above, the celebrated album *Bluesbreakers: John Mayall with Eric Clapton* (1966). Early sessions included recordings for Marianne Faithfull with producer Andrew Loog Oldham and session guitarists Jimmy Page and John Paul Jones, later of Led Zeppelin.

His first co-production credit came in 1967 with the debut album of Ten Years After. A year later, encouraged by Rolling Stones manager Andrew Loog Oldham, he left Decca to found his own production company. He worked on all the classic recordings by Elton John, including such hits as 'Your Song,' 'Rocket Man,' and 'Goodbye Yellow Brick Road'. Dudgeon's role in Elton John's success should not be understated. Elton trusted him. Gus said:

> Once Elton had done what he had to do, which was play the piano and sing, he left. Whatever you hear on the records that's over and above the essential construction of the song is down to myself and whoever else was working in the studio.

(*Billboard*, 26 April 1997)

In 1969, he produced David Bowie's first hit, 'Space Oddity', and later, albums by such artists as Chris Rea, Lindisfarne and XTC.

In 1962 Gus was sharing a flat with Roger Pettet at No. 2 Lymington Mansions in West Hampstead. Pettet, who worked as a stagehand at the BBC, said that Long John Baldry slept on a bed in the hallway. At the time, John was singing with Alexis Korner and Cyril Davies Blues Incorporated, which included Jack Bruce, Dick Heckstall-Smith and Charlie Watts. Davies then set up the Cyril Davies All Stars and when he died in 1964, Baldry took over as leader of the band. Roger also remembers hearing John with Rod Stewart on Eel Pie Island. This was followed by the band The Steamhammer, who Roger thought were one of the most exciting bands of the time. He saw them several times at Klooks, which was just down the road from their flat. Tragically, in July 2002 Gus Dudgeon and his wife Sheila were killed in a car crash.

Roy Thomas Baker, Engineer and Producer

At the age of 14 Baker started work as an intern/runner at Decca Studios working with skilful engineers such as Bill Price (The Sex Pistols) and Gus Dudgeon. Although Baker admits that this was an incredible training ground for engineering, his heart and truest talents lay squarely in production.

> I always wanted to be in record production, and engineering was a pretty good route, although, at that time, it was actually far more difficult, especially in England. Now it seems like a natural step — you become an engineer and then you become a producer, but it doesn't always work out. A lot of engineers can get really good sounds, but it's their rapport with artists that is the thing that is most important.

(*EQ*, 2001)

Baker left Decca and moved to Trident Studios where he produced records for The Rolling Stones, David Bowie, The Who, and Queen, among many others.

Tom Allom, Engineer and Record Producer

Allom, looking back on his experience at Decca Studios, said:

> I had no formal training at all, and I became a record producer as a sort of natural progression from being a recording engineer. I had done a holiday job at Decca Studios in 1964 - it was a magical three months - all sorts of future stars came flooding through there that year, including Jimmy Page, Ginger Baker, Jack Bruce and Tom Jones.
>
> When I walked into Decca studios in 1964, there were these great big valves - the size of milk bottles - in the back of the desk, and The Bachelors were recording Ramona. About every ten minutes, the session came to a grinding halt and all these fellows in lab coats and hushpuppies came in with soldering irons. The console looked like it came out of a Lancaster bomber - and it probably did! They finally got rid of it. I think somebody threw it off the roof!

(*Music Journal*, 2002)

In the 1970s and '80s, Allom worked with Genesis, Black Sabbath, and The Strawbs.

Peter Sullivan, Producer

In 1970, after producing many hit records for people like Johnny Kidd, Lulu and Tom Jones, Sullivan left Decca and along with producers George Martin, Ron Richards, and John Burgess from EMI, formed the independent record company AIR (Associated Independent Recordings). The gamble paid off and Decca and EMI let AIR produce many of their records.

Kevin Daly, Engineer and Producer

Daly began work at Decca in 1957 as an office boy. He moved up to a progress chaser, then assistant engineer and producer. In 1963 he and his wife lived in No. 159 Broadhurst Gardens, one of the adjoining properties which Decca Studios had bought. Kevin said:

> Decca in those days was clearly a friendly, happy place to be, with a nice crowd of people. The inside of the studio building itself was often described as submarine-like: long corridors on different levels, large pipes along the walls; there were a myriad of doors opening onto editing rooms, transfer rooms, and of course, the three main studios themselves. The new Studio 3 was a long way from the front door – the whole length of the Decca submarine. Studio 1 was straight ahead as you entered the building, its control room high above the studio, accessible by a steep flight of stairs; Studio 2 was downstairs, and was the most intimate, and the most modern in feel.

(*The World of Kevin Daly* by his son Michael Daly. www.kevindaly.org.uk)

Derek Varnals, Engineer

Derek worked at Decca for seventeen years on all the classic recordings by The Moody Blues. He also was the recording engineer for artists such as John Mayall, Tom Jones, Lulu, Keef Hartley, and Thin Lizzy. When the studios closed in 1981 he became technical adviser to the British Phonographic Industry, and in 2007 he was awarded an MBE for his services to the recording industry. The magazine *Sound On Sound*, July 2009, printed a very good article about Derek's work when recording 'Nights in White Satin' and the album *Days of Future Passed.*

Tony Clarke, Producer

Tony Clarke was one of the architects of symphonic 'prog rock' through his work with The Moody Blues. With Derek Varnals he worked with the Moodies on six more albums, helping them to become one of the most commercially successful bands of the time. He recorded with a wide variety of acts, including The Equals, the Irish folk band Clannad, and Rick Wakeman. He was very proud to be one of the few white producers to work on a Motown record when he was asked to produce The Four Tops in 1972.

Born in Coventry in 1941, in his teens he was playing bass in a West Midlands skiffle group, and then various local beat groups. By 1963 he got a job in London with Decca, first working in promotions and then in the production department, under Dick Rowe. He started work as a producer in 1965. He achieved success when he produced The Equals' 'Baby Come Back', which went to Number 1 in 1966 and launched the career of Eddy Grant. At the same time he produced his first LP, a live recording by John Mayall's Bluesbreakers. On the strength of these successes, Clarke was given the task of reviving the fortunes of fellow Midlanders The Moody Blues, who had scored a Number 1 hit in 1965 with 'Go Now', but whose subsequent singles had failed to break into the Top 20.

Decca had set up the Deram label as a showcase for its latest developments in stereo sound and the initial plan was for The Moody Blues to record a rock version of Dvorak's *New World Symphony*. The concept was soon rejected. In its place, the Moodies and Clarke assembled *Days of Future Passed*, featuring original songs by the group and grandiose orchestral arrangements played by the London Festival Orchestra, together with the symphonic electronic sounds of the Mellotron. When it was released, British record buyers were initially taken aback by the transformation of an R&B group into symphonic prog rockers, and the album barely scraped into the Top 30. The US was more open-minded and the album shot to Number 2 in the Billboard chart. The album also produced two hit singles, the million-selling 'Nights In White Satin' and 'Tuesday Afternoon'.

Clarke worked with other acts but the increasing complexity of The Moody Blues' recordings was soon taking up almost all of his time, to the extent that he effectively became the sixth member of the band. The group's next two albums, In *Search of the Lost Chord* (1968) and the chart-topping *On the Threshold of a Dream* (1969) were so successful that The Moody Blues established their own label, Threshold Records. Clarke left Decca, effectively to run Threshold, and took the lead role in building the group its own studio in the old Decca studio, Studio Number 1. Clarke died on 4 January 2010, aged 68.

THE END OF DECCA STUDIOS

On 21 November 1981, the English National Opera took over the Broadhurst Gardens building. Now called Lilian Bayliss House, it is used for rehearsals and as offices. Decca moved into No. 254 Belsize Road, Kilburn, where they set up an editing and copying facility rather than a recording studio.

This chapter has given a selection of the thousands of artists who recorded at Decca Studios in Broadhurst Gardens and contributed to the huge catalogue of records produced there between 1937 and 1981. Decca played a significant role in the history of popular and classical music recording, and many music fans consider the quality of their recordings to be remarkable. But in recent years, their achievements have been overshadowed by EMI at Abbey Road, partly due to the continuing popularity of The Beatles. Rock tours of London regularly take in the famous pedestrian crossing outside the EMI Studios, but Decca's contribution has largely been forgotten.

2

THE RAILWAY HOTEL AND WEST HAMPSTEAD TOWN HALL

This chapter looks at the history of the Railway Hotel and the West Hampstead Town Hall, the two buildings which housed Klooks Kleek and Decca Studios.

As the 1870s drew to a close, the Hampstead fields west of Finchley Road, until recently 'the domain of the timid hare', were about to undergo a radical change. In his *Records of Hampstead*, Frederick Baines said:

Railway Hotel in 2008.

> A new district takes the name, none knew how, of West Hampstead. West End Lane transforms itself into a brand new London street. Beautiful and costly houses spring up right and left. Finally, domiciles by hundreds spring up in all directions.

On 14 May 1880, Richard Pincham was granted a provisional license to sell alcohol at the Railway Hotel, which he intended to build on West End Lane. His plan was to create a public house, incorporating accommodation and space for hire, at the corner of Broadhurst Gardens. Pincham was keen to do everything he could to exploit the potential of the developing neighbourhood, by offering an up-to-date venue for travellers and locals alike. In the first week of January 1881, the *Kilburn Times* reported that while some work still had to be done, the Railway Hotel was open for business. Two years later it offered:

> Accommodation for railway travellers, good beds, private sitting rooms.
>
> Grill room, chops and steaks at any hour. Dinner parties, large or small, catered for on the shortest notice. Billiards, pyramids and pool. Good stabling.

Pincham had acquired two blocks of land facing each other across West End Lane and in addition to his hotel, he built two rows of shops with living accommodation above, which he called Exeter Terrace. He was soon joined by two other developers, Thomas Bate and Edward Bailey, who were responsible for building a great many houses in the neighbourhood. Thomas initially set up as a grocer and tea merchant in Kilburn and moved on to property speculation. Edward was a carpenter by trade who married Thomas's widowed sister, Cecilia. Both men built business premises and workshops on Broadhurst Gardens, round the corner from the Railway Hotel. Their Falcon Works (originally No. 2 Broadhurst Gardens) provided space for woodworkers, plumbers, painters and locksmiths. In August 1884, the *Kilburn Times* reported that employees of Messrs Bate and Bailey had met at the Works to enjoy their annual 'beanfeast', or work's dinner.

This was destined to be a short-lived enterprise, however. Bate experienced financial problems throughout his business career. This time he may have had family or health issues; he had been seriously ill a couple of years ago. In April 1884 the local press reported he was about to resign from his many parochial duties. The Works building was empty by October of 1885 and offered for sale the following year. The new owner was butcher Henry George Randall, who had a shop at nearby No. 2 Exeter Terrace. A local paper reported that he wanted to convert the Works into a Town Hall for West Hampstead. The article also noted that in doing so, Randall was carrying forward the original idea for the Works, which were built with a view to provide the neighbourhood with a local meeting place. Despite Bate and Bailey's commercial occupation, it could be true – Thomas Bate had his finger in many local pies, which included an earlier and similar project. His Kilburn Town Hall, in nearby Belsize Road, opened about 1876, and was intended to provide the neighbourhood with a local venue for concerts, meetings and other social gatherings.

The alterations to transform the Works from a business premises into a public hall were carried out, but Randall wasn't satisfied with the improvements. He embarked on a second and massive programme of renovations and alterations, such that the local paper was able to report in October 1891: 'The (Town Hall) is now very compact and convenient, and well suited for a variety of purposes.' All the cloakrooms and artistes' dressing rooms had been redecorated. There were now two halls; the larger, with its splendidly polished pine floor, had been updated by the addition of five large 'gas stars' with a number of tinted lights on the walls. A smaller hall had been created at a lower level, also well-lit and warmed, that could seat 300. Randall also created what he called a 'capital promenade' under the main hall, furnished with garden seats. Finally, and to comply with LCC requirements, he added two fire escapes. The building was renumbered as No. 165 Broadhurst Gardens, and duly embellished with the description 'Town Hall' on its imposing triangular stone pediment. The words 'West Hampstead' appeared beneath, and a coat of arms (origin unknown) was added and still remains today.

A single three-storey house with a bay front (later No. 167 Broadhurst Gardens) occupied the site between the Railway Hotel and the Falcon Works. It may have been quickly modified; as photographs show the entire ground floor was removed to permit the storage of carts, and the whole building was used as a jobmasters and livery stable. Its original

A Victorian advert for Taylor and Lown.

purpose was to serve the Railway Hotel, but by 1900 it had become a branch of Taylor and Lown. The hotel link was maintained, progressing from stabling horses to garaging for cars by 1926. It was then called the Railway Hotel Garage.

West Hampstead Town Hall

Despite their titles, this hall and its Kilburn counterpart were never local government offices. Their function was a purely social one – a building anyone could hire. While the losses incurred in running Kilburn Town Hall contributed to Thomas Bate's final bankruptcy in 1895, West Hampstead Town Hall produced a fairly steady income for its owner. The *Kilburn Times* had earlier, in 1884, extolled the virtues of the neighbourhood, reinforced by subsequent house building:

> Rich in natural attractions and admirably served by three railway companies, West Hampstead has now become the chosen rendezvous of a population both numerous and select. The transformation of 'West-end' which was nothing but a quiet rustic nook, into 'West Hampstead', is one of the most remarkable changes to be found in any London suburb.

The Fleming family moved to a newly built house in Narcissus Road, off Mill Lane, in November 1899. Their son Charles recalled that his parents regularly used the shops in Exeter Parade and the short length of Broadhurst Gardens round the corner. He remembered concerts at West Hampstead Town Hall. The building was intimately involved with the lives of the new residents, by offering space that could be hired for social and official gatherings. The smaller function rooms of the Railway Hotel performed a similar role, and the range of activities that took place there gives an insight into how community life developed and how tastes changed with the passing years.

Dinner at West Hampstead Town Hall, c. 1921.

Schools hired the Town Hall for concerts and prize-givings, while organisations as varied as the Boy Scouts and the North West London Motor Cycle Club held their meetings there. In some instances, congregations held services at the Town Hall before their church or synagogue was completed. Concerts and plays were performed to large and appreciative audiences. For example, in December 1895 the celebrated musician Senor Zerega brought his Spanish troubadours to West Hampstead. The promotional material made much of the fact that the 'world-renowned mandolinists, guitarists, singers and dancers' had twice appeared before Queen Victoria.

An original (and by today's standards unacceptable) farce entitled *The Black Boarder* was staged at the Town Hall in April 1898. Written by Horace Johnstone, the plot centred on a boarding house, where Prince Jab-a-Jab Singh, a sham potentate, made love to the lady guests, proposed to them all and stole their jewellery. He borrowed money from the male boarders before being finally unmasked. In 1902 and 1903, the Merrymakers' Club (whose vice presidents included such well-known personalities as Charles Wyndham, A.W. Pinero, George Sims and Clement Scott) performed 'before a large audience over-flowing the hall'.

The West Hampstead Town Hall was well known on the lecture circuit, and hosted regular talks on a wide range of subjects. Charles Richardson (5 February 1890) enthralled the audience with 'Ireland: its scenery, songs and celebrities', while Sir Richard Temple (12 March 1890) spoke on a weightier and almost certainly less entertaining topic, 'The Coaling Stations of the British Empire'.

In 1905, Captain Jack Claus Voss stopped off at West Hampstead during his UK tour. With the help of some 'beautiful original lantern views', Voss recounted his amazing 40,000-mile sea voyage – his attempt to circumnavigate the world. It was an undeniably brave endeavour and his expertise ensured the survival of his craft in many storms, when, according to Voss, his patented sea anchor played a key role in stabalising the boat. However, the official story excluded some of the facts about Voss and the man with whom he planned the voyage, Canadian journalist Norman Luxton.

On 20 May 1901, Voss and Luxton set sail from British Colombia on board the yacht *Tilikum*. It began life as a 38ft-long Indian crafted canoe made from a cedar tree, the name *Tilikum* being the Chinook word for 'friend'. It cost $80 to buy and the deal was sealed with a bottle of rye whisky. The canoe was refitted before the voyage: the sides were built up and a lead keel, three masts, a deck and a small cabin were added, plus a load of ballast. The yacht successfully made it to the Cook Islands by September but Luxton abandoned the voyage the following month. The journalist was exhausted; he had argued with Voss and alleged that he (Voss) had threatened to throw him overboard.

It took another three years (and several changes of mate) before *Tilikum* made harbour on the Thames. Walter Louis Begent, who was Luxton's first replacement, fell overboard and was drowned en route from Fiji to Australia. Voss had to navigate the 1,200 miles to Sydney without his compass, which Begent had been holding when he fell. Luxton later said he was sure that Voss had got drunk and thrown Louis overboard.

After a prolonged stay in Australia, Voss resumed his voyage in 1903 and reached South Africa in December. From there, *Tilikum* sailed across the Atlantic to Brazil, finally arriving at Margate on 2 September 1904, where Voss was welcomed by a 500-strong crowd. Unfortunately, the voyage didn't count as a circumnavigation as the final leg to British Colombia was abandoned. Voss published *The Venturesome Voyages of Captain Voss* in 1913; Luxton's notes were edited by his daughter and *Luxton's Pacific Crossing* finally appeared in 1971.

The *Tilikum* was put on display at Earl's Court in the months following Captain Voss's talk at West Hampstead. It is now in the Victoria Maritime Museum in British Colombia, Canada. After several joint publicity appearances in Australia, Luxton never saw Voss again. He returned to Canada where he went into business; he died in 1962. Voss returned to the sea, working in the Japanese sealing industry. He was supposedly employed as a bus driver when he died of pneumonia in Tracy, California, in 1922.

There were more sombre events at the Town Hall. In May 1899 a recital was held in aid of the *Stella* Relief Fund. The *Stella* was a railway steamer that made regular sailings between Southampton and Guernsey. On 30 March that year (the Thursday before the Easter holiday weekend), the voyage was busier than usual. En route, *Stella* encountered several banks of fog and was travelling fast, possibly racing another boat. It hit a submerged reef off the Channel Islands and sank in just 8 minutes, with the loss of at least 105 lives. As there was no passenger manifest, the exact number of fatalities was never determined. Later, the well-intentioned *Stella* Relief Fund was defrauded by some of its administrators.

At 7.41 a.m. on a foggy November day in 1907, two workmen's trains collided on the Metropolitan Railway at West Hampstead station (today's TFL Jubilee line). The first train smashed into the back of the second, which was waiting at the platform. Many fatalities were anticipated, and the *Illustrated Police News* of 2 November 1907 said, 'it had been decided that the West Hampstead Town Hall should be opened for the temporary accommodation for the injured.' In the event, the scale and nature of the injuries - three killed and a dozen injured - meant that the hall was not needed.

Several inquests took place in the more intimate setting of the public rooms of the Railway Hotel. One of the earliest was held a few months after the hotel opened, in August 1881, when a verdict of accidental death was returned on 8-year-old Harry Tombs, the son of the stationmaster at the local Midland Railway station on Iverson Road.

Two Watneys drays, each drawn by three horses, were delivering beer to a pub near West End Green. Several boys were playing close by and it was alleged that one of them gave the driver some apples in return for a ride, once the delivery had been completed. A few of the boys climbed onto the drays while others ran behind, as the wagons went off at a trot down West End Lane. Harry was swinging on a chain at the back of the first cart when he dropped his school slate. He tried to pick it up but fell onto the road and the wheels of the second dray went over him, crushing his head and stomach. George Tombs, Harry's father, was in his garden when he heard shouting. The poor man picked up his son and took him home. Harry died the next morning but not before he told his father he could have got out of the way but had wanted to save his slate, which had a lesson written on it.

The Railway Hotel was also used for auctions of property, as local estates came under the hammer and were sold in lots for building purposes. In 1885, the Kilburn firm of Baker and Son sold fifty plots on the Woodbine estate (on Fortune Green Road) and six plots in Sherriff Road. For their convenience, potential purchasers were advised the hotel was close to the Metropolitan railway station.

The Town Hall was an excellent venue when matters affecting the wider community had to be discussed, such as a meeting on 21 February 1891, when the Manchester, Sheffield and Lincolnshire Railway proposed to build a railway line through Hampstead, terminating at St Marylebone. Political parties often hired out the hall, and in 1913 speakers at a Suffragette meeting met with a very mixed reception, when the evening was disrupted by a group of students. It was planned that Mrs Emily Pankhurst would be present, but the chairwoman, Mrs Dove-Willcox, gave Mrs Pankhurst's apologies: she was exhausted and particularly concerned for her daughter Sylvia: 'We have reason to fear that Miss Pankhurst is being forcibly fed inside Holloway Prison.'

Instead, Mrs Flora Drummond, a leading member of the Women's Social and Political Union, chaired the meeting. Imprisoned nine times for her work to further Women's Suffrage, she was known as 'The General', after her habit of wearing military uniform to lead processions astride a horse (at the time, side-saddle was *de rigueur* for ladies). Mrs Drummond was heckled but she was used to dealing with interruptions. Next, a large amount of 'electric snuff' was scattered in the hall by the protesters. (The active ingredient in this alarming sounding substance was acridine, which induced violent sneezing and streaming eyes.) Although scores of people were affected, they were willing to tolerate this irritant. However, when the noise made by a large rattle brandished by a student 'brought upon him the ire of a lady behind, who aimed at him a blow with her umbrella', chairs were overturned and thrown in all directions. The students formed a square and wrestled with the stewards: 'Many blows were struck and when eventually there was a lull in the disorder several persons were seen to be nursing injuries.' Mrs Drummond's parting shot was, 'I have a son, and I hope he will never degrade womanhood like you have done!'

British Pathé has a 1913 film of Mrs Drummond picketing the home of politician Sir Edward Carson.

War was declared in July 1914, and the following year a military band playing stirring music and a guard of honour, made up of eighty fresh recruits, marched to Broadhurst Gardens to encourage others to volunteer for a new brigade of artillery, the 'Happy Hampstead Howitzers' as the mayor called them:

> A number of splendid recruits boldly ascended the platform amid rounds of cheering and applause and announced their readiness to enlist in the 183rd Hampstead Howitzer Brigade (Royal Field Artillery).

According to the Mayor, there were additional perks:

> The uniform was undoubtedly attractive, and he had been told that it 'fetches the ladies'. (Laughter and applause.) The work associated with horses and guns was intensely interesting, the pay was better, and artillery had not to look forward to those long, dreary, and dangerous hours in the trenches.

Conscription to the forces was introduced less than a year later.

Only three years after the end of the war, public interest in the fate of the large number of wounded and disabled servicemen was waning. Yet it was estimated that in the London area alone there were over 7,000 soldiers still in hospital, and probably three times as many out-patients. The Adair Wounded Fund was set up by Basil Frederick Leakey. Born in Hampstead in 1882, Basil became a company director, with a second career as a talented conjuror, under the stage name of 'Alan Adair'. In 1921 he worked out a scheme to entertain wounded soldiers at a series of concerts and dances. The aim was to provide 'a continuous round of pleasure' for the soldier patients, who were invited guests. Leakey selected several central London venues, including the Wigmore Hall, the Alhambra and the Palladium. In 1926 and 1927, the Adair Wounded Fund also hosted several socials and dances at West Hampstead Town Hall (but it didn't attract the star turns of the West End events, which included an appearance by Sophie Tucker). These charitable events were among the last to be held at the Town Hall before it became a recording studio. The Adair Wounded Fund went on to entertain soldiers injured in the Second World War. It was finally wound up in 1958 and Leakey died the following year.

Richard Pincham and Henry George Randall

Both these entrepreneurs were successful self-made men. They were among the first of many traders who opened businesses catering for the new and rapidly growing community of West Hampstead. And in the case of Randall, he arrived in the area about 1881 and stayed until his death, over thirty years later.

The Pincham Family

Richard Pincham's father, Thomas, was an omnibus proprietor in Wandsworth, South London, where Richard was born in 1842. The 1861 census has Richard living with his widowed mother who was working as a nurse, while he was employed as a pawnbroker's assistant. Richard married Ann Wilkinson in 1868, but as the daughter of a labourer, it is almost certain she brought no significant cash to the relationship. The major and unexplained change in Richard's status occurred during the

1870s. By 1877 he'd become a pawnbroker in his own right and a man with money who decided to invest in property. Property speculation was probably the key to Pincham's financial success. In the 1881 census, Richard was living with his wife and son above the Railway Hotel, where he described himself as a 'builder and licensed victualler'. Presumably this was an indication of his current priorities.

Dealing with drunk customers is part and parcel of a publican's work, but in the early hours of 24 May 1885, Richard was surprised to discover 20-year-old George Wilmot in the private living quarters over the bar. It was 2.30 a.m. and Wilmot seemed to have a plausible reason for being there: he told Pincham he'd been tipsy and fallen asleep downstairs, and was now trying to find his way out. But Richard noticed Wilmot had removed his shoes, to make as little noise as possible. Pincham promptly sent the young man downstairs, locked him in the parlour, and blew a whistle to summon help. It arrived promptly, as the Railway Hotel was just a few doors away from the West Hampstead Police Station. Wilmot was charged with burglary after a broken windowpane and slipped window catch were discovered.

Pincham's standing in the community was good and he was elected to serve as a vestryman for the Kilburn ward during the 1880s (equivalent to a local councillor today). Due to retire from his vestry duties in 1887, Richard appointed a manager to run the Railway Hotel and by 1890 he had left West Hampstead for Hastings on the Sussex coast. He took over the Old Golden Cross hotel and public house in Havelock Road, while his wife Ann opened a boarding house next door. Like the Railway Hotel, Richard's new premises were close to a railway station, in this case on the main line serving Hastings.

In 1896, Pincham sold the Railway Hotel to West Hampstead estate agent Ernest Owers, whose office was next to the Metropolitan station. Richard died in London the following year. It is possible he had been too good a host during his years as a landlord, as the cause of death was cirrhosis of the liver, which is often caused by prolonged drinking. The census returns after Pincham's departure show the Railway Hotel had a large number of live-in employees. In 1901, six bar staff shared the accommodation with a porter, billiard marker and waiter, in addition to the manager and his wife. The manager and licensee was not necessarily one and the same person. The hotel continued to offer all the usual facilities of a public house in addition to providing a pleasant venue for parties in the public rooms above the bar. In 1929 the local Criminal Investigation Department (CID) and the Hampstead Ramblers both held their annual dinners there, with more than enough space for entertainment. A 1933 advert described the facilities on offer:

> The Railway Hotel. (Mrs L.J. Gabbett). Restaurant Service. Luncheons 12 to 3, large parties especially catered for; evening dinners arranged; Dance Hall, 'Broadhurst Rooms', well appointed, available for concerts, clubs, parties etc.

By 1934 the hotel was the property of R.V. Goodhew Ltd. Started by Rudolph Goodhew and later taken over by Watneys, the company owned a chain of public houses and restaurants. In October 1936, the Hampstead Rotarians held their annual dinner in the Broadhurst Rooms, so functions were still being catered for. But Goodhew's advertising was basic and to the point, with the entry for the local directory in 1937 simply stating: 'The Railway Hotel Public House.'

Henry George Randall

Henry came from a large family and was born in Buckinghamshire in 1847, where his father John was a farmer. John moved to London soon after; the 1861 census shows 14-year-old Henry had left home and was working as a live-in butcher's assistant. In February 1871 he married

Annie Maria Stallibrass, and after several years spent as a ship's provision chandler in Gravesend, Kent, Henry moved back to Hampstead to work for his brother Thomas. Thomas had a butchers' shop on Englands Lane and another on Haverstock Hill, where Henry was made manager. From there Henry moved to West Hampstead and started his own business: a brief mention in the *Kilburn Times* of 14 October 1881 notes his shop was about to open at No. 2 Exeter Terrace. His brother Joseph was also a butcher and each developed their own 'territory': Henry's was West Hampstead and Finchley Road; Thomas served Belsize Park and Hampstead, while Joseph's shops were in Highgate and Crouch End. The brothers prospered and it was said of the family: 'The name of Randall is possibly one of the best known in connection with the butchering trade of London.'

Henry was familiarly known as 'Uncle Nutty', or just plain 'Nutty' to his business associates. According to the son of a local West Hampstead tradesman:

> Randall always wore a Muller-cut-down tilted over his left eye, a brown tweed tail-coat of country style although no doubt it was made by an expensive West End tailor, and a button hole. He had the reputation of being a man about Town.

This was in marked contrast to his domestic circumstances, for Henry chose to live modestly over his shop in West End Lane for the rest of his life. Not only was he successful in his chosen trade, but he also engaged in profitable property speculation, often working with Ernest Owers.

His shop at no. 239 Finchley Road opened in the 1890s and replaced his first premises nearby, which was demolished when the railway to Marylebone was built. A butcher's shop was still trading at no. 239 and using the name H.G. Randall as late as 1954.

Number 239 Finchley Road in about 1905.

Henry died in 1924 aged 77, West Hampstead Town Hall was put up for sale as the year drew to a close. *The Times* for the 6 October advertised the 20 November auction:

> The West Hampstead Town Hall
> Broadhurst Gardens, NW. Substantial property.
> Licensed for music and dancing. Held for about 57 years at a ground rent of £20 per annum. Vacant possession.

In 1928 the Crystalate Manufacturing Company Recording Studio moved into the building and set up their studios.

The Railway Hotel in the 1950s and '60s

During this period the pub was owned by Watneys and leased to R.V. Goodhew Ltd. Although it was still a hotel, it didn't offer rooms to the public – all the upstairs accommodation was for staff only. On the ground level there were three bars and a restaurant, complete with waitress service. Lunch was served on linen tablecloths for the princely sum of 5*s* 6*d*. In the basement was another bar known as The Dive. On the first floor was a ballroom with a bar and cloakroom – this was the space later used by Klooks Kleek.

In 1955, Patrick Linnane, who supplied this information, was transferred from The King's Arms, Edgware Road, to be the assistant manager at the Railway Hotel. He told us that the ballroom was used occasionally for dinner dances. The clientele was mixed: cards and dominos were played in the public bar, while the middle bar was used mostly by dustmen and coal men; the lounge bar attracted office workers and managers, with a good sprinkling of staff from the next-door Decca Studios.

After a short period at another pub in Richmond, Pat Linnane came back to run the Railway Hotel in 1959. In the corner of the restaurant was an old piano. He had it cleaned, tuned and paid a man £1 to play on Saturday and Sunday nights, which was popular with the customers. When Pat built a stage, hired a singer and bought a microphone, it was a big success. The Rotary Club hosted a lunch in the ballroom every Tuesday and Pat had the brainwave of using the space for wedding receptions. Following one occasion when a wedding party had difficulty in getting a band, Pat thought if he could provide music, a photographer, a cake and a wedding car, he could offer the complete wedding service – all that was needed was the bride and groom! Before he knew it, he had a wedding booked every Saturday afternoon and a dinner dance from 7.30 p.m. until midnight.

Another popular weekend was the England-Scotland rugby match at Twickenham. Two coaches of Scottish fans would arrive at 7 a.m. on Saturday morning and they would be shown into the Railway Hotel for breakfast in the ballroom. This really impressed the neighbours! They were then piled onto coaches to the match; after the game they returned for the dinner dance, which usually finished at 1 a.m. on Sunday.

Dick Jordan and Geoff Williams approached him about using the ballroom as a club. Pat decided to take a risk and he operated the bar on the first floor. To begin with, business was quite slow, but it soon took off when it became an R&B club. Pat remembers numerous bands, including Georgie Fame, who played the club on many occasions, and after the release of his hit record 'Yeh Yeh', there were long queues and people had to be turned away. Pat left the Railway Hotel in 1966 but continued in pub management for another ten years. He spent the last eighteen years of his working life at the Royal National Theatre in Waterloo, retiring to his native Galway, where he still lives today.

Just before Pat left West Hampstead, the *Kilburn Times* of 12 March 1965 printed an article on the Railway Hotel. On the evening the reporter visited, there were three elderly tenors singing an Anglo-French song probably well known to the First World War troops. One of the singers, 65-year-old Sidney McDonnell, said he had been coming to the Railway Hotel since 1918. The second tenor was 56-year-old Albert Martin, and the third of the trio was Ernie Fisher, who was 67 years old. Young people drinking in The Dive bar in the basement said they liked the pub because it was nice and quiet. Pat told the reporter he had a very good crowd of regulars. His only complaint was the 1,872 spirit glasses taken by patrons over the year. At two shillings each, this represented a considerable loss of profit. The paper reported that after four years, the popular Klooks Kleek jazz and R&B club, which was held in the first-floor ballroom, had a membership of 15,000.

3

KLOOKS KLEEK

This chapter could not have been written without the help and cooperation of Dick Jordan and Geoff Williams.

THE BEGINNING OF KLOOKS KLEEK

Klooks Kleek was a jazz and blues club at the Railway Hotel, which ran from 1961 to 1970. The story of the club involves two childhood friends, Dick Jordan and Geoff Williams, who grew up in wartime St John's Wood. They lived in Alma Square and were in the same class at Barrow Hill Road Primary School. As Geoff said:

> The 20 minute walk to school permitted lots of imagined war games, touring of bombed buildings against all injunctions of parents, teachers and air raid wardens, and occasionally getting caught out in the open during bombing raids.

After secondary school Dick joined the screen advertising company Pearl & Dean (who many people will remember from their cinema adverts) as a trainee cameraman.

Geoff worked briefly for Mobil Oil before completing two years National Service with the RAF in Germany. After demob and a summer of washing dishes in Joe Lyons, he joined the Ministry of Agriculture, Fisheries and Food. For his work in international development, Geoff was awarded an OBE in the 1998 Queen's Birthday Honours.

Geoff and Dick at the Pearl & Dean car rally. (Johnnie Morrice)

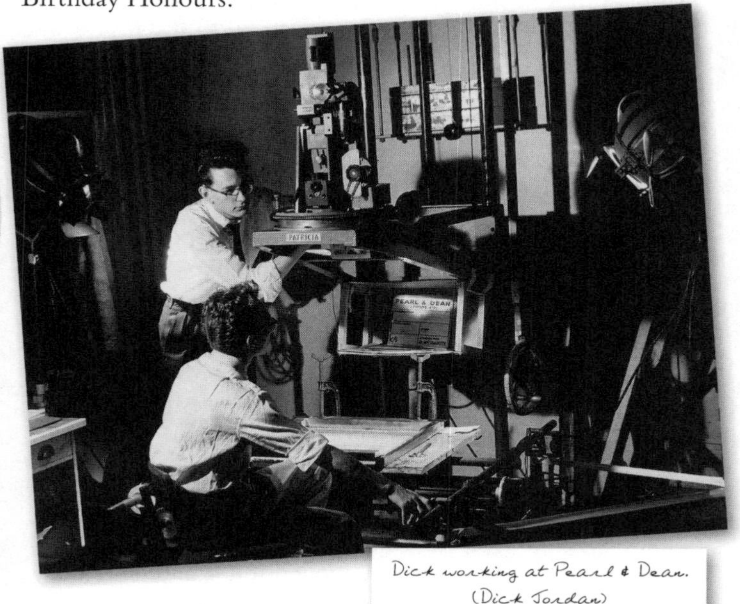

Dick working at Pearl & Dean. (Dick Jordan)

Dick learned to play the trombone in his teens and he took a few lessons from Eddie Harvey, the trombonist with the Johnny Dankworth Seven, but it wasn't good news:

> Eddie's analysis was clear and simple; I would never ever make it as a competent amateur trombonist and we were both wasting our time as well as my money. Apparently I'd travelled too far without proper tuition and had got myself into non-returnable bad habits. However that unfavourable criticism didn't deter me from continuing to play in four bands.

The first band Dick occasionally sat in with was a trio, plus vocalist Mike Thompson, who Dick described as a 'Frank Sinatra copyist who'd be perfect in a counterfeit Rat Pack.' They had a residency at The Ivy Club, an establishment in Kensington which resembled the club shown in *Dance with a Stranger*, the film about Ruth Ellis who was the last woman to be hanged for the murder of her lover David Blakely. Dick talked about the other bands he played with:

> By now I had bought myself a 1938 Fordson van, fitted with ex-trolley bus seats on either side and I was able to obtain more gigs because of supplying the transport. A 'trad' band called 'The Neolithic Jazz Men' hired me because of my van, my trombone playing was obviously secondary. Amazing as it now seems, I knew many vehicle-less drummers and bass players who knowingly bought their instruments and just relied on taxis, public transport or scrounged lifts from people like myself, luckily, some paid for my trombone plus petrol. The trumpet playing leader of this band was Adrian Lynne, an advertising film director who shared with me many cinematic anecdotes about the film industry. He eventually moved to LA and directed; 'Indecent Proposal' and 'Nine and a Half Weeks'.

Dick's main band was The Central Jazz Unit, a modern jazz group born out of Pearl & Dean, where the alto sax player and Dick were employed in the camera department. The rest of the band worked as artists in a studio in Marylebone Lane specialising in boot and shoe catalogues. Dick was also in The Mike Martin Band, which played a wide range of music.

Mike Martin band. (Dick Jordan)

Mike, who had a job in the music department of Harrods, also ran a club at The Six Bells pub in Chelsea's Kings Road and another at the Red House pub near the St John's Wood roundabout. Mike advertised his band and clubs on the Harrods staff notice board which attracted the attention of the daughters of high society who were 'slumming' it at Harrods for a few months to gain some work experience. The band played a few society functions and hunt balls, including a private party for Princess Margaret. Dick remembered the occasion:

> It was the time when cha cha cha was sweeping the country and a feature number of the Mike Martin band was 'The Peanut Vendor'. At the party Princess Margaret took to the dance floor with her partner and the other guests politely faded away leaving the Princess cha cha chaing to my trombone solo. I thought, eat your heart out Eddie Harvey!

The Mike Martin Band, with Dick Jordan on trombone. (Dick Jordan)

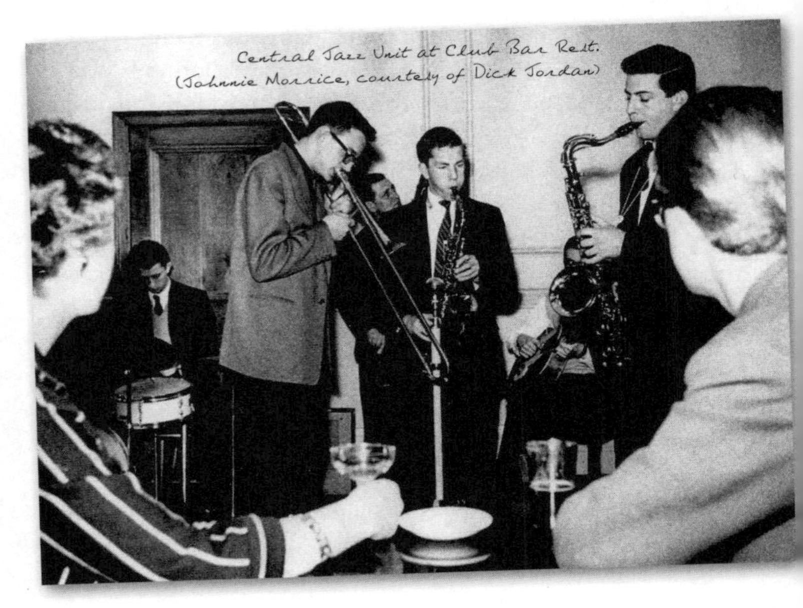

Central Jazz Unit at Club Bar Rest. (Johnnie Morrice, courtesy of Dick Jordan)

These clubs gave Dick the idea of starting his own jazz club featuring The Central Jazz Unit and they opened at the Red House in September 1958. The report in the *Marylebone Mercury* uses the typical 'beat' language of the time:

> Six cool cats of the modern jazz world sat down in a room over the Red House Inn, St John's Wood, on Sunday and had themselves a ball. As their instruments ripped out shattered melodies, discreet red lighting gave glimpses of 40 'hep' teenagers jiving wildly. And the new Central Jazz Unit was under way. Started in the days skiffle was all the rage, the Unit was determined to stay modern. 'Man we can't play a waltz or foxtrot, and as for that skiffle ... ' drawled leader Dick Jordan. 'This is our first night, but we are doing all right; must be over 40 here already.'

Dick left Pearl & Dean the same month his club opened, to work freelance on several films until he joined Presbury Films in Soho at the beginning of January 1959. He said:

> I worked on 'Robin Hood, Robin Hood, riding through the Glen' and other feature films that are now totally forgotten.
>
> Although Presbury Films is generally unknown, it was they who introduced the world to cinema advertising. In the 1890's when insurance companies forced theatres to lower the safety curtain during the interval, the curtain was covered with painted advertisements. Old man Presbury suggested painting a white space in the centre and projecting ever changing lantern slides displaying local shops. And one thing led to another.

The club at the Red House lasted for just seven months before Dick was given notice to quit the premises because it was being replaced by a Hilton hotel (now the Danubius).

The last Sunday gig was held on 26 April 1959, to the great disappointment of Geoff, who had heard about the club in a letter from Dick and was looking forward to going there after demob. But Geoff's demob was in May 1959! Dick looked around for new premises and remembered singer George Melly inviting him to a Decca live recording at the Railway Hotel, a pub where the location and layout were perfect for a club. (The recording was made in May 1957 and released as 'Mick Mulligan and his Jazz Band, Live with George Melly'.)

At the outset, Dick's arrangement was for a six-week trial with a rental charge of three guineas a week, rising to six guineas if the contract was extended. The first night was 4 May 1959; but it was a difficult time to start Club Bar Rest, as he jokingly called the new club:

> In the hot summer of 1959 the sales of ice cream, beer and day trips to the seaside increased significantly. Attendances at cinemas and jazz clubs were on the other hand significantly down on the previous year, so it wasn't the perfect time to open 'Club Bar Rest', in what proved to be the hottest summer since 1933. With film locations taking me out of town and with the rest of the Central Jazz Unit living south of the river, I just couldn't handle the regular running of the club on my own. With low attendance figures of twenty five or so, it became a waste of time and a liability, so I let the club die a death. The band disbanded and then, without me, joined forces with another band whose drummer was Charlie Watts, who soon left to join the Rolling Stones.

So the doors closed in September 1959. But Dick still believed that a club with a resident band and top-line guest musicians could succeed:

I was trying to get a band together with Glen Hughes [who at the time lived locally in Lymington Road, West Hampstead], a young baritone sax player who impressed the jazz critics with his smooth tone and fluid style. I had played a few gigs with him at the 'Ivy Club' and was amazed by his virtuosity. We never got any gigs together and I gave up when Glen joined the John West Group, a quartet which played every Sunday at the 'Crown' pub in Twickenham. Glen invited me to see the band and immediately the idea of opening a club with a more 'professional' stance looked a reality.

So Dick started Klooks Kleek on the first floor of the Railway Hotel, where there was a large banqueting room for the band to play, as well as a separate lounge bar. Held every Wednesday night, it began as a modern jazz club reflecting Dick's love of the music:

I booked the John West Group as the resident house band at Klooks and by adding a different named guest each week, a varied approach could be achieved. Our opening night on 11 January 1961 featured Don Rendell, a top British sax player, as the main guest. The 'Melody Maker' sent along a reporter and 'The Kilburn Times' sent a photographer and reporter.

Klooks Kleek opening night poster. (Dick Jordan)

The *Kilburn Times* of 20 January 1961, reported the opening of the club:

> Jubilant modern jazz fans flocked to the 'Railway Hotel' in West End Lane on Wednesday evening last week for the opening of a new Mecca in the world of contemporary music. Called somewhat inexplicably – the Klooks Kleek, it is the only club in North West London which offers top class modern jazz for a reasonable price. The entrance fee is half a crown and membership a shilling. The person behind it is a young cartoon film cameraman, Dick Jordan of Alma Square. Slim and bespectacled he has long held the conviction that there is a big demand for a club such as Klooks Kleek in this part of London. 'We've already got over 200 members' he said happily. Dick Jordan has apparently no ambition for profits. Despite excellent attendances at the club's first two evenings he has only just managed to break even. When I suggested that the admission price might be raised once the club is better know he replied resolutely, 'No, I'm going to keep it at 2*s* 6*d*. This must be a club which everyone can afford.'

ORIGIN OF THE NAME KLOOKS KLEEK

Many people have wondered where the unusual name of Klooks Kleek came from. As Dick explained:

> People have forever asked me how I came up with the name Klook's Kleek. I'd read somewhere in a film magazine that George Eastman, the inventor of Kodak film and cameras believed the letter 'K' to be the ugliest letter in the alphabet and yet it's an easy letter to pronounce. On a page of print a single 'K' will stand out from the rest of the type. Eastman came up with the word Kodak which

has two K's. A 1956 jazz LP by the drummer Kenny 'Klook' Clarke entitled 'Klook's Clique' grabbed my attention and by changing the spelling of Clique to Kleek I could have four K's and they really do stand out.

The unique atmosphere at Klooks was down to Dick's ingenuity:

With all the centre light chandeliers switched on there was a lack of atmosphere. If I switched some of them off there was an unbalanced area of gloom so I decided to switch them all off and place side tables around the entire club area. They were covered with red gingham table cloths with table lamps and orange coloured bulbs. That would warm the dark side of the club and give a comforting glow. Our spot lights were effective and cheap. They were made from large, empty Fox's Glacier Mint tins. The lids were unscrewed and the centres cut out, coloured gels could be held in place by screwing the lids back on again. Spot light bulb fitments were soldered into the ends of the tins, handles were soldered onto the body of the tins and by fixing them to the walls with G clamps you had effective spot lamps.

From a contact in the film business I obtained two powerful 20 inch speakers from a demolished cinema and with an aircraft carrier's high wattage amplifier that was being sold by an Army surplus store in Soho's Lisle Street, so a great sound system was installed. We also had a professional Ferrograph tape recorder playing Sinatra style music in the club bar (you must remember this was 1961 when Ol' Blue Eyes was riding high). In the foyer there were large coloured back-lit florescent display units announcing future attractions. The policy was to provide good jazz, including two bands, for listening and dancing and with an entrance price of just 2/6*d*, how could it fail?

In the early 1960s, jazz mainly attracted a young male audience, and for the club to succeed, Dick knew he had to widen its appeal:

> Providing there was good jazz on offer which was never known to be a great crowd puller, the financial success of the club would be reliant on the number of women that visited the club. With a strong emphasis on jazz for dancing I needed the support of the resident band to keep their's and the guest's solos to a minimum length. More happy women would attract more happy men.

Dick also tried to attract more women to the club by having women musicians and some free or half-price nights for women. So, for example, he booked the wonderfully named Helen May Strip, a sax player with the all-women Ivy Benson Band. But knowing how her name would attract jokes, she was simply billed as 'Helen May of the Ivy Benson Band' on 19 April 1961. Kathy Stobart, another very good sax player, played several times at Klooks. The plan succeeded and membership increased steadily.

Val Simmonds (back to camera), and friends at a crowded Klooks Kleek in around 1962. (Val Simmonds)

Val Simmonds, who worked in PR in the music business and whose husband, Harry Simmonds, was the manager of the band Chicken Shack, said that Klooks was *the* place to hear good music, and she and her friends became regulars there.

JAZZ AT KLOOKS

Most of the leading British jazz players played at Klooks in its first few years. This was the time of the 'Beat' generation and sax players were the most popular performers in the 1960s.

Ronnie Ross

Dick talked about sax player Ronnie Ross:

> Another early guest was Ronnie Ross, the baritone sax player who later featured on Lou Reed's 1973 hit single 'Walk on the Wild Side'. In 1961 I booked him to play Klooks and advertised it as a 'Battle of the Baritones' with our own Glen Hughes. The two baritone saxes battled it out and Ronnie exclaimed to me how good Glen was. A vote wasn't taken but it was generally agreed that an amateur baritone sax player won the battle that night.

Geoff added, 'Glen said to me at the end, I got the old bugger waggling his arse in the last number.'

Glen Hughes

When Glen was 18 he played with John McLaughlin (guitar) and Rick Laird (bass). In a 1978 interview John recalled:

> Rick Laird and I went back to the days when I had a trio with a baritone player, Glen Hughes ... We had such an incredible relationship as friends, and as musicians we had fantastic rapport. We used to do Jimmy Giuffre/ Jim Hall things; and Chico Hamilton; Miles; and Sonny Rollins tunes.

(*The Guitar Player Book*, 1979)

In February 1963, Jet Harris and Tony Meehan, previously the bass player and drummer with Cliff Richard and The Shadows, had an unexpected Number 1 hit record called 'Diamonds'. On the strength of this they recruited a band which included saxophonist Glen Hughes, a young John Paul Jones (later of Led Zeppelin) and guitarist John McLaughlin, who formed the Mahavishnu Orchestra in 1971. Tony Meehan said:

> We were doing the sort of things which Chicago and Blood, Sweat and Tears came up with a few years later. But we were booed off stage with some of it, the mainstream jazz things. People didn't want to listen, they just wanted to bop. It was dancing days - you didn't listen to music.

(Alex Reisner's Led Zeppelin site: ledzeppelin.alexreisner.com)

There are a number of West Hampstead connections here; as a child Tony Meehan lived in Sidney Boyd Court on West End Lane, and he was at Kingsgate Primary School with one of the authors, Dick Weindling. Tony Meehan then went to secondary school at Regents Park Central in Lisson Grove, where Dick Jordan also attended. Another local connection is that at one time John Paul Jones lived at No. 7 Priory Road.

By 1964, Glen was part of Georgie Fame's very successful band, The Blue Flames. In 1966, Glen tragically died in his flat in Shepherds Bush. In his autobiography, fellow sax player Dick Heckstall-Smith (who lived in West Hampstead) said:

> Glen died in bed with a cigarette in his hand, drugged unconscious with smack. Glen was, in my opinion, one of the best baritone players the world has seen.

(Dick Heckstall-Smith and Pete Grant, *Blowing the Blues: Fifty Years of Playing British Blues*, 2004)

Dick Jordan, who was a good friend of Glen, said:

> When Glen was living in Lymington Road he often popped up to the club on his days off and once told us how he'd just made his easiest buck in a recording studio just by playing a few notes. Georgie Fame had just recorded 'Get Away' his 1966 single where at the end of each chorus there's a single note played on Glen's baritone sax. Whenever I hear that record I always think of Glen and what a wasted death.

Dick Morrissey

Dick Jordan talked about his first meeting with Dick Morrissey:

> On Klooks opening night Glen Hughes introduced us to a young shy tenor player we'd never heard of before and neither had the featured sax player Don Rendell. With a three sax line-up the jazz was blowing free and exciting our new inquisitive audience. Don was obviously impressed by this young tenorist making him work hard to keep up and he asked Glen where this unknown had been hiding. 'Ireland' replied Glen. Don gave lessons to Glen and he always encouraged enthusiastic young musicians.

The shy young man was Dick Morrisey and he played at Klooks more than twenty times during the next three years. Geoff said of him:

> He was easily the most popular, with audience and fellow musicians alike, of the regular performers at Klooks Kleek. Dick went on to success in jazz-rock with If and The Morrissey-Mullen band. He died, aged 60, in 2000.

The band If was formed in 1969 and (with changing personnel) lasted until 1975. The Morrissey-Mullen band began in New York City, where Dick Morrissey and Jim Mullen

Glen Hughes with Dick Morrissey, 1961. (Kilburn Times, courtesy of Dick Jordan)

(guitar) were recording and touring with their friends in the Average White Band and Herbie Mann in 1975. 'M&M', as they were called, were very popular on the club circuit. But Dick Morrissey's health problems led to the break-up of the band in 1988.

In the 1970s, Dick Jordan was the agent for If, The Average White Band, and another popular jazz rock band, Ian Carr's Nucleus.

Tubby Hayes

Tubby Hayes was the leading British sax player during the 1960s. He first played at Klooks on 1 November 1961 and then a further six times. Geoff said that Tubby was:

> THE star of British jazz from the 50s to his death in 1973 at age 38. Tubby and his group filled the club on every appearance, except the one when a London pea-souper enveloped the City and the evening consisted of a quiet beer with the promoters and vibes player Bill Le Sage, and the discovery that the pub owned piano was out of tune with itself, would have prevented him playing the vibraphone!

Tubby was born in south London as Edward Brian Hayes in 1935. His father was a violinist with the BBC Revue Orchestra and Tubby learned to play the violin and piano at an early age. He played with numerous jazz bands during the 1950s; fellow sax-player Ronnie Scott remembers the first time they met:

> I was playing at a club near Kingston, and was asked if I minded if a local player sat in: This little boy came up, not much bigger than his tenor sax. Rather patronisingly I suggested a number and off he went. He scared me to death.

Scott was very impressed and later he and Tubby, who both played tenor sax, co-led the highly praised Jazz Couriers. During the 1960s, Tubby had his own band until serious illness resulted in major heart surgery in 1969. He tried to make a comeback but needed further surgery in June 1971. Tubby continued playing until taken ill in Brighton in 1973. He died in Hammersmith hospital. Ronny Scott told *The Times*, 'He was the best jazz musician this country has produced, and quite probably the best it will ever produce.'

Klooks Kleek was going well and on 25 May 1962, the *Kilburn Times* carried an item which said that Klooks had reached 3,000 members. The 3,000th member was presented with an LP gift. The paper noted that 'Klooks Kleek is a young, progressive and eager club and supported by young and enthusiastic people. Long may it stay that way.'

Dick was confident that the club would succeed. In 1962, while doing some film work, he impressed Ted Moore – a very talented cinematographer – who offered him a job on a film called *Dr No*, working in Jamaica for six months. Dick turned it down and also another offer to work on a film called *Lawrence of Arabia*. By now, Klooks had established itself and Dick did not feel he could walk away. Ted Moore later worked on six more Bond films and a host of other well-known films.

KLOOKS HOUSE BANDS

Looking back many years later, Geoff talked about the quality of the house bands that accompanied the top of the bill jazz performers:

> Amongst their leaders were Brian Auger when he still had a day job, and the classically-trained Manfred Mann, who had arrived from South Africa in its dark days, as a modern jazz enthusiast. Never a shrinking violet, Brian added energy and wit to his formidable musical skills as a performer often introducing numbers in a Harry Seagoon voice or interrupting Dick's announcements with Goon Show noises. One always thought there was another Dudley Moore itching to emerge from the chrysalis. But music was his business and he was to have considerable success with his own amplified Trinity, The Steampacket and with Julie Driscoll. Manfred moved from jazz to

bluesy pop, with a group that included Paul Jones, Tom McGuinness, and Jack Bruce. Manfred took up residence in the charts from 1964 to 1969, and then again in the mid-70s with his successor band Manfred Mann's Earth Band. Both the Earth Band and The Manfreds (most of the originals except Mannie), continue to tour today.

A regular house band was the Dave Morse Quintet which consisted of Dave (vibes), Stewart Williamson (bass), Chick Andrews (drums), Brian Auger (piano) and Wally Houser (sax).

Dave Morse was an industrial photographer at Napier Aero Engines in Acton where coincidentally Dick's grandfather had worked as chief engineer during the First World War. Dave later became a commercial photographer.

Dick recalls the story about Stewart's classy girlfriend who introduced him to her parents. When Mummy asked Stewart what car he drove, Stewart confidently told her it was a Rover. 'Oh, how super,' she said, 'and what year?' Ashamed with owning such an old car, Stewart replied '1938'. There was a prolonged silence as Mummy added, 'Oh, never mind, it *was* a good year.'

Chuck 'Chris' Andrews refused point blank to take a drum solo. He had a very respectable day job and under

Dave Morse band on West Hampstead station. (Dick Jordan)

Dave Morse Quintet at Klooks in around 1962. Notice how close the audience is to the band, which was part of Klooks' intimate atmosphere. (Val Simmons)

no circumstances could the name 'Chick' be mentioned. He was an enthusiastic weekend cricketer and Geoff's club agreed fixtures with his team. Unfortunately it contained about nine West Indians at a time when every young man of West Indian origin was either a power-hitting batter or thunderbolt bowler, or both. So Geoff and his team got several thrashings, while Chick wore a contented smile.

Brian Auger was the mainstay of the group and the only member to continue as a professional musician. Any vocalist being accompanied by Brian Auger was delighted by his versatility in playing in any requested key. Apparently he gained experience while on tour with Sarah Vaughan who would agree a key and then change it mid-song without any warning.

Wally Houser was a solicitor for Ronnie Scott's club and also for Dick and Geoff's company Jazz Contemporaries.

Dick remembers a time when Wally brought his friend to the club; her name was Christine Keeler but at the time they didn't know who she was until she hit the headlines in the Profumo Affair in 1963.

Wally regularly opened the jazz nights with a fifteen-minute spot before the star of the evening came on. His favourite tune was 'Satin Doll' and he played it very well, particularly his solo. The only problem was that one or two Klooks regulars were unshakeable in their belief that every week his solo was identical, note for note. One of them, an angry Irishman, came out front one night and, having failed to find Dick, demanded that Geoff instantly pull Wally off stage and stop using him. 'Much as we believed in involving the members in the club,' recalls Geoff, 'this was a bit too far, not least because Padraig and his mate were the only people to complain.'

To extend interest for club members and gain publicity, Dick and Geoff organised a photographic competition in 1962.

The judges were Bob Houston, editor of the *Melody Maker*, who lived locally in West End Lane, and Harrison Marks, a nationally known photographer specializing in nude studies, who lived at No. 66 Redington Road, Hampstead. Dick had met Harrison Marks when he worked on his first feature film, *Naked as Nature Intended* (1961), which starred the models Pamela Green and Jackie Salt. The other judges were also from the film industry; Tony Auguste, stills photographer, Roy Pointer, lighting cameraman, and Brian Probyn, film cameraman.

The winner of the competition received a £10 prize and their photo was published in the *Melody Maker*, 11 August 1962. The winner was Leonard (Len) Karstien. He was an excellent photographer who lived locally in Yale Court, West Hampstead. With Anya Teixeira he formed part of the Hampstead-based Creative Photo Group in the 1960s. His winning entry was a photo of the shadow of baritone sax player Glen Hughes.

Dick, Harrison Marks (holding the cigarette) and Jackie Salt at Klooks. (Dick Jordan)

Len Karstein's photo of the shadow of Glen Hughes, 1962. (Dick Jordan)

In September 1962, the reporter Alec McDonald wrote a piece for *Challenge*, the Young Communist League journal. He described his summer visit to Klooks:

> Heavy curtains black out the evening summer sun and one enters as though into a cave. Orange and red tamps give illumination. Orange and red 'spots' dye the bandsmen … Soon past eight the four rows of straight-back chairs are filled. The occupants are serious students of modern jazz: rapt faces, bodies inclined in concentration. The tables fill with young men and girls, faces flushed by the table lamps. Animated, strong-beat music a background to animated conversation. Around eight-thirty the chairs set along the walls are nearly all occupied. Soon the build-up of newcomers flanks the jive-area – yet empty – with a unity of jumpers and jeans; twist dresses and beehives; suits and leather jackets. A boy and girl begin jiving sedately alone. A few more couples take the floor, three, four, five, and within minutes a crowded floor.

Membership continued to grow and in January 1964 Tubby Hayes presented an LP and life membership to the 10,000th club member. There was a very successful night in August 1964 when The Polish Modern Jazz Quartet played at Klooks. Geoff said:

Cartoon of Dick and Geoff by 'Sandy'. (Dick Jordan)

> Led by altoist Zbigniew Namyslowski the quartet gave a sensational rendering of progressive jazz. They played again by popular acclaim the following month.

Despite this success, maintaining enough interest in the jazz night was proving difficult. Rock and roll, The Beatles and the growth of the blues had all affected the popularity of modern jazz. The 17 October 1964 issue of the *Melody Maker* included an interview with Dick Jordan, who said:

Some areas where entertainment is restricted, or there are poor train services, can get away with using non-name groups. At a place like Klooks Kleek, where they can get to the West End for an extra shilling we can only put on the best. The fans are getting very fussy. They study the *Melody Maker* club columns before deciding where to go. But it's not just the music that's important. Two clubs in my area had to close because they had the wrong atmosphere. The right atmosphere is created by a combination of things like the music, lighting, comfort and whether the groups get them dancing. We are trying to find something which appeals to people who don't like R&B and don't like discordant modern jazz because it isn't raving enough.

HEREZA KLUB THAT'S THRICA WEEK

Mondays'n'Tuesdays - Rhythm'n'Blues Days 3/6 (5/- Mose Allison & Memphis Slim)

Wednesdays - Modern Jazz Days 3/- (3/6 Polish Modern Jazz Quartet)

MONDAYS IN AUGUST - 8.15 - 11.00

10th Ronnie Jones and the Night Timers
17th Great American Blueser
MOSE ALLISON
24th John Mayall's Bluesbreakers
31st Ronnie Jones and the Night Timers

TUESDAYS IN AUGUST - 8.15 - 11.00

11th John Mayall's Bluesbreakers
18th Graham Bond Organisation
25th **MEMPHIS SLIM**

WEDNESDAYS IN AUGUST - 8.15 - 11.00

12th Johnny Scott and Duncan Lamont
19th Tommy Whittle and Ken Wray
26th **Polish Modern Jazz Quartet**
featuring Zbigniew Namyslowsky (alto)

YOUR STARS FOR THE FUTURE

September 21st GEORGIE FAME
„ 28th LITTLE WALTER
October 12th JOHN LEE HOOKER

Railway Hotel, West Hampstead

Due to Licensing Laws, no one admitted under 18

h Legs - Free Toilets

Advert for the Polish Modern Jazz Quartet, 1964. (Dick Jordan)

The 'something' he was talking about was the idea of having a duo with a singer and a sax player, which Dick and Geoff thought would be popular. The jazz singer Bobby Breen worked with either Dick Morrisey or Danny Moss on sax, but after five gigs audience numbers were still too low to continue. So after almost four years, jazz at Klooks came to an end. As Geoff said, 'The change of style did not attract a large enough audience to sustain Wednesday night jazz and it ended on 11 November 1964.'

The *Melody Maker* for 14 November 1964 carried a piece on the closure:

> The latest London club to give up the unequal struggle after four years of trying to sell modern jazz is Klooks Kleek. Dick Jordan is sad about the whole affair.
>
> 'We have tried a number of things. Instead of the resident trio and guest artists we tried using different bands. We had people like Tubby Hayes, the Polish group, Eddie Thompson, and Dick Morrissey. Lately we tried mixing blues and modern jazz, using Bobby Breen and Morrissey. Attendances have just dropped every week. You literally can't give tickets away – I know, I've tried. I used to subsidise the jazz evenings from the R&B sessions … People at the club are still coming up to me and saying they like modern jazz and asking me not to drop it, but what can we do? We have been losing between £15 and £20 a night, and for us that is a lot of money.'

Dick tells an interesting story from this time:

> On the last jazz night of jazz, Brian Auger's bass player, Lennie Williams asked for my advice or a second opinion. He'd been offered a recording session, playing bass, on a one-off single and wasn't sure whether to take a straight fee or a percentage of record sales. My first reaction on

discovering that the studio was in a dodgy part of West Kilburn, was that established recording studios generally operated in a nice part of town, well they did then! Added to that was the name of the female vocalist, which didn't bode well so I advised Lennie to take the session fee route. Even if the record proves to be a success, you can't guarantee you'll get your royalties paid. Lennie heeded my advice.

When I later discovered the record company set up, I was pretty miffed at the advice I'd given to Lennie. The studio belonged to another unknown, Chris Blackwell, who had proven himself to be a man of integrity and a knowledgeable source on Caribbean music. He discovered Bob Marley for a start. The unknown vocalist turned out to be Millie and the record, 'My Boy Lollipop', sold millions. Lennie never gave me a hard time over my advice because primarily it was his decision and responsibility. He left the jazz scene soon after and became a bassist with the Liverpool Philharmonic orchestra.

In 1964, Millie Small's recording 'My Boy Lollipop' reached Number 2 and went on to sell over 7 million records for Chris Blackwell's Island Records. Their office was at No. 108 Cambridge Road, on the Willesden side of the Kilburn High Road.

R&B AND BLUES AT KLOOKS

In the meantime, in an attempt to get more customers through the door, Dick and Geoff decided to introduce a R&B night on Tuesdays and increase membership to 1*s* 6*d*, which also included the jazz night. The first band to play on 10 September 1963 was Georgie Fame who alternated in the opening four months with Graham Bond and the Wes Minster Five. This was the turning point for Klooks: as Dick put it,

'The change over from modern jazz to R&B was immediate and financially viable.' He and Geoff were in the right place at the right time to catch the popular demand for R&B.

Dick talked about events leading up to the opening night:

> In January 1963 The Beatles released their second hit single, 'Please Please Me'. In February it topped the New Musical Express charts and they four handedly changed the face of popular music world wide, including Klooks Kleek. Modern jazz was already on the wane as Rhythm and Blues began replacing it as an exciting alternative.
>
> The first night we ran R&B, in the autumn of 1963, Georgie Fame and The Blue Flames were topping, supported by our resident interval band led by Manfred Mann. When he'd asked if his jazz quintet could support Georgie Fame during the interval, I wasn't sure if Manfred's music would fit into the R&B mould. But they'd already rehearsed new R&B numbers for this eventual day and by changing their name for the occasion to the Manfred Mann Blues Brothers they soon became a big success with Number One hits. When the doors opened on the first night, there was a lengthy queue down Broadhurst Gardens and for the first time we had to close the doors. The change over from jazz to R&B was extraordinary in that many of same jazz crowd came to see Georgie Fame out of curiosity for the first time and were hooked.

The Tuesday session was the main R&B evening and this continued until Klooks finally closed on 27 January 1970. Because of its success Dick and Geoff added a second R&B night, which began on Monday 13 April 1964 and ran for a year. This was later replaced by Thursday soul nights and a more dance-oriented approach, which ran from 1 April 1965 to 6 November 1969.

Georgie Fame

Georgie Fame was very popular with audiences and he played over twenty gigs at Klooks. He also played in the jazz slot on 21 August 1963, and as Geoff said:

> Despite his R&B tag, fans were delighted to find the repertoire included Louis Jordan, Cab Calloway, Fats Waller and Charlie Parker numbers. Manfred Mann's band was also on the bill.

Georgie, real name Clive Powell, was born in Leigh, Lancashire, in 1943. After playing piano in local bands and at Butlin's Holiday Camps, Georgie came to London in 1959. He was signed by well-known agent Larry Parnes and worked as singer Billy Fury's accompanist in 1960 and 1961. Parnes, who was born in 1929 at No. 98 Christchurch Avenue, Brondesbury Park, gave stage names to most of his acts, including the singers Tommy Steele, Vince Eager, Billy Fury, Duffy Power and Marty Wilde. Parnes decided that Powell would be his house pianist under the name of Georgie Fame. The career of Georgie Fame, blues and jazz singer, would take another couple of years to develop.

Georgie Fame at Klooks Kleek, around 1963. Notice the 'famed' Klooks' table lamp, part of the cosy atmosphere of the Club. (Dick Jordan)

In March 1962, Georgie and the band The Blue Flames started playing regularly at the Flamingo Club in London's Soho district with Georgie on a Hammond organ. A Number 1 hit came in January 1965 with 'Yeh Yeh' and was followed with 'Get Away' the following year. He has worked with a wide variety of musicians, including Count Basie, Eric Clapton, Muddy Waters and Hoagy Carmichael. Georgie tells good stories about the time he asked Hoagy to clear an album of Carmichael covers made by Georgie and other British musicians. Suffice to say he earned the approval of the great old man as well as a giant hangover. As Geoff said, Georgie was, and still is, extremely popular as a live performer.

Dick remembers when they thought about starting the R&B nights:

> Before we opened the R&B nights and to get some idea of how successful Georgie Fame and The Blue Flames were at attracting large crowds at The Flamingo Club, Geoff and I often went to see the band in action. We intended doing big business with Georgie's agent and manager Rik Gunnell. The Flamingo had become infamous with its All Nighters and was an unlicensed all night club of sorts and lost little trade because of it. By selling a bottle of Coke with an illegal slug of Scotch for 10 bob the crowd could get satisfyingly sloshed with the added attraction of being part of a speakeasy (Godbolt, *A History of Jazz in Britain* 1989). If you wanted to eat, there was a choice of Chinese takeaways across the road in Gerrard Street.
>
> Geoff and I were concerned that the R&B we'd be promoting at Klooks, known as 'Sax/Organ led R&B' attracted a more volatile clientele as opposed to the 'Guitar led R&B' which attracted under 18 year olds and was unsuitable for a licensed pub with the old West Hampstead 'Nick' (police station) next door. We couldn't help notice that The Flamingo did possess an aura of violence and Rik Gunnell, an ex-boxer and ex-Smithfield meat porter, who was always present as one of his team

of bouncers, wasn't prudish about lifting his shirt to show us his knife scarred belly. 'A knife doesn't frighten me; a gun – is a different matter.' We had to face it, Klooks would require bouncers.

KLOOKS AND THE KRAYS

The 1960s were the time when the notorious Kray twins ruled the London underworld and made money by operating 'protection deals' with various clubs. Dick tells the story of how close he came to the Krays in 1967:

Johnnie Buccheri had been my Soho barber for thirty years and he was a friend and a regular member of Klooks Kleek. His Sicilian father had arrived in Britain around 1900 and opened a barber shop in Soho's Macclesfield Street, a link road between Shaftesbury Avenue and Gerrard Street. The Krays had their offices just around the corner in Gerrard Street.

Johnnie always insisted on customers making appointments and surprise, surprise, when I arrived one day, bang on time, there sitting in what should have been my chair was one of the Kray twins (which one I don't know). Johnnie's other two barbers were not there, they were either taking a late lunch, off sick, on holiday, or more likely staying away to avoid having to cut the twin's hair. Johnnie ran a busy shop and I would guess he had further appointments following mine, but this Kray insisted on waiting until his favourite barber became available, so, unless there was a cancellation Johnnie would be busy until closing time while one of the Kray twins sat in his barber shop making it appear that Johnnie hadn't paid his 'protection'. As Johnnie began cutting my hair, the Kray joined in our conversation and nosily asked what I did for a living.

For my own safety's sake I was about to say I worked in the film business, but before the words came out, Johnnie blew it by introducing me as a club owner. Running a club above a Watney's boozer didn't in my mind elevate my status as being a club owner, unfortunately, the Kray recognised this as an opening gambit and I added hastily that Klooks had no gambling license, no restaurant, all the booze sold was the sole property of Watney Ltd and the club was next door to the West Hampstead police station.

Catching the Kray's reflection in the mirror, I noticed his eyes widen as he demanded to know Klooks' address and then touched my arm as he quietly assured me he'd be coming up to see me. Johnnie told me later that he reckoned there was no way the Krays would be interested

Dick and Geoff with the security staff (in around 1965, photographer unknown). From left to right: Harry Bowles; 'Babyface'; Geoff Coxon; Pete Davis; Bill Slack; John Maule; Geoff Williams; Dick Jordan; and Mick Pretty. Geoff would like to point out that he is not a midget: the others are standing on beer crates. (Dick Jordan)

in Klooks Kleek as it was a small time club that wouldn't fit into their big league operations. But I wasn't convinced.

About a month later, Johnnie happened to be talking to me in the Klooks foyer when he pointed out two dodgy characters entering the club with their ladies. He whispered to me they were a renowned pair of Soho villains who occasionally did the odd job for the Krays. Johnnie thought they may be checking out the club's credentials on behalf of the Krays, but whatever they were doing they were potential trouble. An A.P.B. went out to the bouncers to stop any disturbance that arose around them and not to get involved with them. They went off to the bar and returned later to see one of their ladies dancing with another man, who was then hit full in the face. The bouncers were close at hand and able to control the incident from spreading while the villains left the club. We weren't sure if they were representatives of the Krays or just passing through. I know one thing, I was grateful that Johnnie was at the club and had warned me when they arrived and I was very happy that the Krays never moved in on us.

Wes Minster Five

The other regular band in the first months at Klooks was the Wes Minster Five. They were led by Brian Smith (guitar) and included Zoot Money (organ), Jon Hiseman (drums), Dave Greenslade (keyboards), Tony Reeves (bass) and Chris Farlowe (vocals), all of whom went on to play in other bands.

Zoot Money

Zoot Money with his Big Roll Band was a very popular performer. They played at Klooks thirty-four times between the 3 March 1964 and 10 December 1969. Their New Year's Eve gig in 1965 produced Klooks' highest ever attendance. As Geoff said, 'Few groups achieved the same level of audience response to this mixture of good R&B and George (Zoot)'s larger-than-life personality.'

Zoot and Big Roll Band, 1964. From left to right: Nick Newall (tenor sax); Andy Summers (lead guitar); Colin Allen (drums); Paul Williams (bass and vocals); Clive Burroughs (baritone sax); and Zoot himself (keyboards) holding a camera. (Zoot Money)

NEW YEARS EVE at KLOOKS KLEEK

№

Railway Hotel
West Hampstead

★ ZOOT £ MONEY'S
BIG ROLL BAND

★ 8.30 — 12.30
★ FUNNY HATS and STEAMERS
★ SPOTTY PRIZES WITH THIS TICKET
★ CABARET
★ 10/- TICKET (TICKETS 12/6 AT DOOR)

Klooks advert for Zoot Money, New Year's Eve, 1965. (Dick Jordan)

YouTube has a performance by Zoot at Klooks which, although a poor quality video, captures the excitement Geoff is talking about. This is the only known publicly available film of a band playing at Klooks.

A live recording from 31 May 1966 of Zoot and the Big Roll Band, called simply *Live at Klooks Kleek,* is available on Repertoire Records.

Dick remembered a conversation with Zoot:

> In 1967 Zoot told me his Big Roll Band was now sounding out dated and his days of looning around on stage taking his pants down for a laugh were over. Audiences loved it, but Zoot had had enough. The emerging psychedelic era was posing a threat to his version of R&B and the Big Roll Band metamorphosed into Dantalions Chariot, a light show based band playing underground rock. The first night Dantalions Chariot played Klooks, the giant stage supporting the elaborate light show plus operators at the back of the room was as large as the main stage holding the band. Coupled with the huge P.A. speakers, there was little room left for a large crowd curious to see their re-incarnated Zoot Money and we closed the doors prematurely. The band was on a guaranteed fee against 60% of the box office and with fewer punters, the band barely reached their guarantee. The writing was on the wall, bands would require larger venues to finance their growing road costs and the days of small clubs were numbered.

Zoot appears on a Georgie Fame live recording with his Birthday Big Band at The Forum in June 1998. On the track 'Papa's Got a Brand New Bag', Zoot suddenly shouts out 'Klooks Kleek 1964' as a memory to when he played the song at Klooks.

Looking back at Klooks in 2013, Zoot said:

> Out of so many memorable nights at KKs what stands out ... the band's return from Spain ('66) when for charity, my overgrown hair and beard were cut during the interval, the double band event during which the opening band the Artwood's Jon Lord (later Deep Purple), first used his reproduction Leslie speakers in competition with my two real Leslies. Or of course the recording of the live album, one of the first, I believe, in that room with wires hanging out of the window to next doors Decca – Health and Safety, eat your heart out. Chas Chandler, Eric Delany, and Jackie Trent indicated the diversity of the crowd which was mostly made up of our die hard fans. All suffered the indignity of the random shoe removal during the playing of 'Barefootin'. The tape operator was the late Gus Gudgeon, who from then on got promoted to record producer, doing work for Elton and many others.
>
> Every Klooks gig [was] a happy event, due in no small part to you Dick Jordan, running it in the right spirit.

John Mayall

John Mayall and his Bluesbreakers often played at Klooks. His first session there was on 13 July 1964 and he played a total of thirty-three times over a six-year period. The guitarist with an early version of the band, the late Roger Dean, remembered their gigs at Klooks:

> We used the tiny kitchen area next door to the stage for changing facilities ... There were two rooms upstairs, one in which we used to play, and the room at the front was a bar area. There was also a bit of a problem getting the gear out at the end of the night, if you can imagine trying to carry a Vox AC30 amplifier down a steep flight of steps, and pretending to be sober for John's benefit – not easy!

John Mayall. (Dick Jordan)

Geoff can readily endorse the effect of difficult access to venues. In the early days, a road crew had not been heard of in the UK, they only belonged to US tours. There was a single roadie, with just possibly one of his mates to help, and they'd get into the club for nothing. So Geoff and John Maule, his steadfast front of house assistant, would be beseeched to help carry Hammond organs up a thrity-step flight of steps. The day when someone discovered how to cut a Hammond in two and install connectors between the halves, was a memorable one for porters of gear at Klooks.

Still playing and now living in America, John Mayall had an excellent ear for spotting talented players, and many later famous musicians worked with him. The best known were Eric Clapton and Jack Bruce who, with Ginger Baker, formed Cream.

Graham Bond

The band called the Graham Bond Organisation – Graham (keyboards), Dick Heckstall-Smith (sax), Ginger Baker (drums) and Jack Bruce (bass) – was managed by Robert Stigwood, who also represented many other top bands. He thought that Graham would do very well and said he would buy him a large Hammond B3 organ. Dick recounts the story that Graham told him:

> A happy and confident Graham visited the central London showrooms of Boosey & Hawkes in Regent Street, recognised as the main supplier of Hammond organs for churches, chapels, mission halls and cathedrals. As Graham wandered around the showroom a number of church organists were judging the suitability of which organ was right for them while impressing the small congregation by playing a few bars of Bach cantatas or snippets from the Saint-Sans Organ Concerto. Graham, who could easily have been mistaken for a church organist or minister from an obscure religious sect, didn't appreciate this snobbish and conceited attitude of the customers and quietly sat down at a Hammond B3. He switched on the power, turned up the volume to FULL, put his hands onto the keyboard and began playing 'Wade in the Water'. There was shock horror from the dumbfounded audience as the dark suited salesperson rushed over to Graham demanding him to leave the premises immediately. Even though Graham said he wanted to buy the organ For Cash, he was still dismissed with a pointing finger and told to 'GO'!

On 26 June 1963, a recording of the Graham Bond quartet was made at Klooks by Ray Goganian, who was a successful ladies' hairdresser by day and Klooks' bouncer by night. Three tracks appeared on *Solid Bond* in 1970, with John McLaughlin featuring on the guitar. The rest of the album was nine tracks recorded at Olympic studios with Graham on organ, Dick Heckstall-Smith on sax and John Hiseman on drums, who replaced Ginger Baker after he had formed Cream.

Dick also talked about another recording of the Graham Bond Organisation at Klooks:

> There was a live recording made in 1964 by Graham Bond for what I believed was to be an album. It was in fact an idea of producer, Giorgio Gomelsky, to help Graham

out by recording some tracks for a potential record deal. He brought up a mobile recording deck and then experienced all manner of equipment failures and while he tweaked the knobs he suggested I just keep on talking on the mic to the growing impatient crowd. Believing that the tape wasn't running smoothly I blabbered on and on and made a bloody fool of myself while Giorgio tried to balance the sound. At the end of the session he complained sadly that there just wasn't enough good quality recorded sound material – and that was that. He graciously paid us for the use of our facilities and I remember Giorgio saying that at least Klooks had made some money out of this debacle.

Many years later after Graham had committed suicide and became a minor cult figure, the record was released on Charly Records. In the sleeve notes Giorgio comments: 'Unfortunately the tracks were recorded under extreme difficulty and the quality is lousy.' Critics stated that although the sound is rough and ready it is highly atmospheric. Oddly enough because of insufficient material, track 6 was listed as, 'Introduction by Dick Jordan - a space filler.' It is an embarrassing epiphany of me talking rubbish in conversation with Graham Bond.

Graham Bond. (Dick Jordan)

This recording was reissued in 2006 by Brook Records as *One Night at Klooks Kleek*. Dick's introduction now opens the album before the band launch into a great version of 'Wade in the Water'.

Dick Heckstall-Smith with Graham Bond and Jack Bruce. (Dick Jordan)

Roger Dean, who was the guitarist in the John Mayall band, remembered hearing Graham Bond at Klooks:

> Graham used to stack two huge Leslie rotary speakers one on top of the other, and when the band struck up the whole building would feel like it was about to collapse! Jack Bruce and Ginger Baker were not exactly 'Palm Court' type players either.

Tragically, Graham's drug addiction and mental health problems eventually led him to jump in front of a train at Finsbury Park on 8 May 1974. Harry Shapiro has written an excellent biography called *Graham Bond: The Mighty Shadow* (1992, reprinted in 2005 by The Crossroads Press).

Jon Hiseman

Jon Hiseman played drums with Graham before he set up his own band, Colosseum, in 1968. In his biography, Jon talks about working with Graham at Klooks:

Early one evening, six months or so after he'd left the Organisation, Jon Hiseman got a phone call, out of the blue, from Graham Bond. He was calling from Klooks Kleek (the famous R&B/soul club at the Railway Hotel, West Hampstead). It was about 6 p.m. and Bond was in trouble, his drummer hadn't shown up and would Jon fill in. Though being unwilling to admit it, Jon quite missed the excitement of Graham's musical environment, so with certain misgivings, he loaded his drums in the car and drove to the venue. Later, Jon described that evening as 'one of the greatest playing experiences of my life'. The set kicked off, then as each number segued into the next, they moved seamlessly back and forth through their old repertoire: 'I realised that Graham's ego was driving him to show me just what I had been missing, to catch me out, to lose me, but he couldn't; I knew the repertoire too well and we both began to really enjoy this new adventure. I felt this was my game and we played non-stop for about fifty minutes or so, ending with the inevitable drum solo. It must have been quite an astonishing performance for the audience. People would come up to me for years after and say 'I was at Klooks that night.'

Jon wasn't the only drummer to receive a last-minute panic call from Graham Bond. In a recent conversation with Jon, Keef Hartley related the following story: 'Graham called one night and I too went up to Klooks with the kit. With no rehearsal, I played a set with Graham, all the while cursing you and your bloody technique because Graham was playing all this tricky stuff that you must have worked out with him. After the show was over, the promoter, Dick Jordan asked me if I wanted the money. I thought this a bit strange, but realised Dick must have known by this time that Graham's heroin habit was such, that he had a reputation for not paying the band, which I guess, is why he was being let down all the time. I grabbed the band fee, deducted my share and gave the rest to Graham who immediately shot off into the night to score.'

(*Playing the Band – The Musical Life of Jon Hiseman*, by Martyn Hanson, edited by Colin Richardson, Temple Music, 2010)

Jon Hiseman with GBO. (Jon Hiseman)

Jon also remembered a night at Klooks when his double drum kit began to move in opposite directions, as the crates supporting the stage shifted, but he continued to play while the roadies held the drums in position. For his next gig at Klooks, Jon had an additional clause inserted into the contract to ensure a safe platform!

Dick explained the stage situation:

> When Klooks opened, there were no stage or storage facilities and everything had to be carried up and down the stairs again. But as the pub's beer sales increased and thus improved the Irish manager's standing with Watneys, he offered us some storage space in an unused room. We then constructed five platforms 8ft by 4ft and six inches high. OK, we now had a stage, but it soon became apparent it wasn't high enough for the punters at the back of the room to see. The simple answer was to balance the stages on two raised beer crates. That worked until Jon Hiseman's double drum kit began separating the platforms apart and from then on I spent the first ten minutes under the stage clamping them together.

The Moody Blues

A largely unknown Birmingham group at the time, called The Moody Blues, played during the interval at Klooks on 29 September 1964, when top of the bill band was John Mayall. As the support band they only received a small fee of thirty shillings. Roger Dean said, 'I remember the night we played together with a new group from "Oop North", they were The Moody Blues, and they were excellent.'

The Moodies also supported Sonny Boy Williamson when he played at Klooks at the end of October 1964. They had recently recorded a single, 'Go Now', for Decca which was released in November. But the song, which reached Number 1 in the UK and Number 10 in the US, was followed by several modest years. Then a change in personnel and style led to their big hit 'Nights in White Satin' in 1967. After this the band became one of the leading 'stadium rock' bands of the late 1960s and '70s.

Tom Jones

Because Decca Studios was next door to the Railway Hotel, artists, producers and engineers working there would drop into Klooks. Dick remembers one such occasion:

> Some time in late 1964 two of Decca's in house producers, Mike Vernon and Peter Sullivan, dropped by the club with a Welshman with black curly hair and dark brown eyes. His looks resembled that of a Spaniard rather than a Welshman and although his name was Tom Woodward he didn't sound Spanish at all.
>
> The two Decca boys were on a mission. They were seeking a second opinion on some songs Tom had recorded and needed to tie down a possible single. With a choice of two songs, would Geoff and I plus our six bouncers, give a verdict on what song we thought could be a hit single. When the club closed we went into Decca Studios and listened to the two songs. Unknown to us, Tom's choice was played first, it sounded OK but nothing to write home to Wales about and then came song number two. Wow, the powerful introduction sounded so American big band and immediately grabbed our attention, then in came the vocals and within the next few bars and without even waiting for the track to finish we all proclaimed in unison that this had to be a hit single and possibly a Number 1. Tom still disagreed and believed his choice was the right one, but he accepted the experiment, knowing that the final decision would after all be the responsibility of his manager. Although Tom's surname

> was Woodward, a newly released film starring Albert Finney was fast becoming an international box office hit. Based on an 18th century book by Henry Fielding, Tom's manager decided to rename his new artist after the main character in the film – Tom Jones. I don't remember the name of Tom's chosen single, but the name of the song that we unanimously chose was 'It's Not Unusual' and it certainly did make Number 1 in March 1965.

The recordings were made in Decca Studios on 11 November 1964, and the B side (Tom's choice) was 'To Wait For Love' written by Hal David and Bert Bacharach.

After he became famous, Tom Jones often went into Klooks after recording and although he was recognised by the audience, he wasn't mobbed.

Geoff talked about other visiting musicians from the next-door studios:

> The proximity of Decca Studios was a boon in the regularity with which well-known muso's dropped in and often jammed with whoever was appearing. It seemed that the better-known/more successful they were, the less likely it was that they would expect to enter gratis, whereas lesser lights whose names had appeared once down-page in the *Melody Maker*, would try to blag their way in. Amongst the former group, Mike Smith of the chart-topping Dave Clark Five, seemed almost embarrassed at being waved through. Front of House favourite was a young lady called Marie Lawrie, who expected no favours and even filled in a membership form twice, after losing the first one. She'd already had a Number 7 hit called 'Shout'. Yes, we did let Lulu in for nothing, but we kept it legal with the membership form, and we may even have made a cautionary remark about drinking age, as she was sixteen and a half. The first time she arrived was with

fellow Glaswegian Alex Harvey and his Band, and to the delight of the crowd regularly joined him on stage for a few numbers.

Geno Washington

The exciting Geno Washington and The Ram Jam Band played sixteen times at Klooks in 1965 and 1966, often on the Thursday night sessions. As well as playing his music, Geno owned a restaurant in West End Lane.

Geno told Dick Jordan that he grew up on a housing project in Indiana, Washington. Stationed at an American Air Force base in East Anglia for his military service, he did gigs in London. He immediately felt at home with Britain's liberal and relaxed racial attitudes, and after his release from the Air Force, decided to remain in England. In 1965, with guitarist Pete Gage, he formed The Ram Jam Band with John Roberts (bass), Herb Prestige (drums), Jeff Wright (organ), Lionel Kingham (tenor sax) and Buddy Beadle (baritone). The band was very popular and successfully toured the UK and Europe for a number of years.

Chicken Shack

Gordon Chamley remembers going to Klooks for the first time and the effect it had on him:

> In March 1969 I was a Lancashire lad working in Peckham, South London. My two flatmates were jazz fans and took me with them to Klooks Kleek one evening. Luckily for me there was no jazz on that evening: instead Stan Webb led Chicken Shack in an awesome evening of blues. With an ultra-long teleflex on his guitar Stan wandered through the audience reeling off some electrifying licks. Christine Perfect played piano, and Graham Bond and Jeff Beck also made guest appearances with the band. It opened up a whole new world of music for me, while my two jazz

friends wandered off to the bar in the next room as the music was far too loud for them.

About a year after I first saw Chicken Shack I was inspired to learn guitar and played lead in a local rock band for a short period. In the late '70s I saw Chicken Shack again in a Lancashire country pub called The Lodestar near Ribchester. Sadly there were but a handful of people there (unlike the packed-out Klooks Kleek), but the band still did a great gig and I got to chat with Stan quite casually between sets. Not long after that I emigrated to New Zealand where I have lived ever since. I still have my membership card for Klooks Kleek.

Ten Years After

The very popular band Ten Years After first played at Klooks on 23 January 1968 and then had another three gigs during the year. The Klooks session on 14 May was recorded live and released in August 1968 as *Undead*, their second album. It was produced by Mike Vernon, with cables running into Decca Studios next door.

The summer of '69 was particularly monumental for the band. They were invited to play at the Newport Jazz Festival on Rhode Island and then performed an outstanding set at Woodstock that August. Their rendition of 'I'm Going Home' guaranteed their stardom and they featured prominently on the film and soundtrack album of the Woodstock Festival, which was later released.

Dick talked about the recording of the album and his trip to New York in 1969:

> Ten Years After were playing an open air festival. 'Undead' was in the US charts and riding high. Recorded live at Klooks it utilized Decca's next-door facilities with cables slung across doors and fire escapes. Chris Wright, the band's manager and head of Chrysalis, suggested I introduce the band with the six words, 'Ladies and gentlemen ...

Ten Years After', but the tape machine was hiccupping and Chris asked me to continue for a few seconds until it was fixed. So I rambled on about Cockneys and the L.P. being recorded for the American market, expecting this part to be deleted. But Chris Wright enjoyed my intro and included it on the recording. Later the band ribbed me about how the Yanks loved it. That day in New York I was stunned when the festival's compere introduced Ten Years After with the exact words I had used on their album! At the time I was chatting to Peter Grant, Led Zeppelin's manager, and with little concern he shot across the stage, grabbed the compere saying 'Oih, STOP, the guy who said that is here' beckoning me to come and take over, but by then it was too late, the band were into their first number.

BANDS WHICH DID NOT PLAY AT KLOOKS

Dick Jordan was unable to book some bands to appear at Klooks. Apart from the obvious issue of price and a venue which only held 400-500, the fact of playing in licensed pub premises and the nearby local West Hampstead police station, caused restrictions. In the *Melody Maker* of 17 October 1964, Bob Dawbarn wrote an article called 'R&B: Boom or no Boom?' in which he quoted Dick Jordan:

> In London, the bands can be divided into two distinct groups – those who only appeal to what one might call the kids (say aged 14 to 17), and those who appeal to more adult audiences. The Yardbirds typify the first category. Even if I could afford them, the Yardbirds would be no use to me. They attract the youngsters and my club is on licensed premises.

Other bands which fell into this category were The Rolling Stones and The Animals, although Eric Burdon visited more than once, particularly on Georgie Fame nights. Geoff remembers that once, all the members of The Animals came in. Like the Stones, their roots were in the blues, but they had moved out of the genre into the pop charts; they could not be Klooks Kleek performers because of the age of their fans, and also cost. Another famous band that did *not* play at Klooks were The Who. The confusion occurs because as The High Numbers they played at the Railway Hotel, *Harrow*, not the Railway Hotel, West Hampstead.

THE KLOOK'S ATMOSPHERE

As an example of the different audiences for bands and Klooks' atmosphere, Dick later recalled that on 19 November 1963, Graham Bond was playing Klooks. Down the road at the State in Kilburn, The Rolling Stones were playing to a packed audience of young teenagers. Two Klooks members had been to see the Stones but came away early because the huge number of screaming kids made it impossible to enjoy the band. They said they came up to Klooks for company their own age and the more congenial surroundings.

Chris Welch, a journalist writing to Dick Weindling in 2007, remembered his early days at the *Melody Maker* and visiting Klooks:

> I joined the *Melody Maker* in 1964 and most of my more senior colleagues, including jazz writer Max Jones, editor Jack Hutton, and staff men such as Bob Dawbarn and Bob Houston all lived in West Hampstead or Muswell Hill. In fact Hampstead seemed like the MM's personal

Northern province, which greatly impressed me as a callow youth from the hinterlands of Catford in South London. Many were the jokes about being 'transpontine' – in other words from the wrong side of the Thames. I'd go to MM house parties in Hampstead attended by The Beatles and The Rolling Stones, feeling as though I had entered a fabled land. Here be ultra cool, intellectuals and Marxists who despised the Tories, the royals, and the Establishment but all seemed to deal in shares, drive exotic foreign sports cars and own homes whose values were cheerfully described as 'rocketing'.

But when I wasn't visiting my colleagues' homes – full of cats, jazz LPs and lodgers – I would be going to Klooks Kleek. This involved queuing at the side entrance then going up a flight of back stairs into the room. Here the bands and groups set up. There was no real stage as I recall, and only just enough room for the musicians to squash together with a few speakers and amplifiers. You could easily chat to the musicians who just mingled in with the crowd or headed to the bar between sets. I don't recall them having any kind of star dressing room, bouncers or security men. Not even their managers bothered to show up.

Dick Jordan was well known to my MM colleagues such as Bob Houston and Max as they lived not far away. Dick always announced the bands with a mixture of manic enthusiasm, Goon Show humour and the knowing air of any promoter who hopes to cash in on a successful act's capacity to bring in the audiences. I can remember Dick phoning me at the MM with exhortations to publicise his forthcoming attractions. But most of the time the audiences just seemed to show up – eager to catch the many great live acts of the day.

There were many promoters forever moaning about Klooks receiving regular sound bites in the *Melody Maker*. Dick eased their annoyance by explaining it was down to being a neighbour of many of the journalists. But the real answer was simple, as Dick explained:

> I made frequent trips to the MM editorial offices in Covent Garden with a bottle of Scotch for the journalists (at the time Scotch was more a luxury then than it is today). It obviously worked because Klooks sometimes received weekly mentions and publicity was so important. My neighbour Max Jones told me that 'Klooks was the only club to appreciate the art of giving.'

Dick's Source of Jokes

Dick gained a reputation for his jokes. In fact, producer Gus Dudgeon said on the LP sleeve notes for Zoot Money's *Live at Klooks Kleek*, that Dick Jordan knew more jokes than anyone else he knew. Dick said that he was fortunate to have a very good source:

> I soon began to be recognised as an infinite source of jokes, but the truth is I've never made up a joke in my life, which is not what many people believed. While working in the film business as a cameraman during the day and running Klooks in the evenings, the studio I worked

Dick telling jokes at Klooks. (Dick Jordan)

at in Soho hired all their technicians and stage crew on a daily basis, including all of the electricians who were mostly moonlighting from BBC Television. At that time many shows were transmitted at the weekends but were taped during the early part of the week. Stars who had their own shows such as Harry Secombe and Val Doonican would tell their jokes to camera, say on a Monday, the electricians would repeat them to me on the Tuesday, I in turn would tell them at Klooks during that week and Harry Secombe's joke would be transmitted to the country at the weekend. The following week the club punters would inform me that Harry Secombe told one of MY jokes at the weekend!

AMERICAN ARTISTS

From the summer of 1964, Dick and Geoff began to book American artists. But they were forced to put up the entrance prices, which ranged from 5*s* to 7*s* 6*d*, to cover the larger fees these artists charged.

Dick remembers when Sonny Boy Williamson played at Klooks:

On October 27th 1964 Sonny Boy Williamson, the great American blues singer, played at Klooks and was supported by The Moody Blues. The club understandably was jam packed. Sonny Boy must have been in his 70's and was a wizard with a small harmonica which he slipped up his nose and played effectively by blowing and sucking – what a star. Sonny had no teeth, well that's not strictly true he did have two yellow stumps clinging precariously from his upper gum. So what, he was a legend and we felt proud to have him playing the club. Before going on stage Geoff and I were speaking to him

Champion Jack Dupree at Klooks.
(Copyright Paul Soper, used with permission)

in the dressing room where from his holdall he pulled a litre bottle of Johnnie Walker whisky and insisted we share a drink with him. Why not? Whisky was still an expensive commodity in Britain and austerity was still part of our culture. As he began filling two handy beer glasses, we both exclaimed 'Too much, Sonny.' Sonny Boy simply stopped pouring and moved the bottle over and filled his own half pint glass to the brim. Picking up the glass he boasted that he drank seven bottles of whisky a day. 'Well, that's not quite true,' he added 'I GET through seven bottles of whisky a day. To avoid embarrassment, I share half of it with whoever wants to drink with me.'

On 25 May 1965, when Champion Jack Dupree played at Klooks, he was supported by the John Mayall band, with Eric Clapton on guitar.

John Mayall (keyboards); John McVie (bass) and Hughie Flint (drums) supporting Champion Jack Dupree. (Copyright Paul Soper, used with permission)

Eric Clapton (guitar) and Hughie Flint (drums) supporting Champion Jack Dupree at Klooks, 1965. (Copyright Paul Soper, used with permission)

On 1 February 1966, the 15-year-old Stevie Wonder played the drums and sang with a backing band called The Sidewinders, which included pop singer Dickie Pride. Stevie was then billed as Little Stevie Wonder. Dick and Geoff were a little concerned about his safety on the makeshift 'stage'. He had his first American Number 1 when he was only 13 years old and his musical career and huge success continue today.

Other US artists who played at Klooks included Memphis Slim (August 1964), Mose Allison (August 1964), Buddy Guy, supported by Rod Stewart's Soul Agents (March 1965), T-Bone Walker (March 1966), Ben E. King (November 1966), Bo Diddley (April 1967), John Lee Hooker (June 1967), and Jose Feliciano (June 1967).

Roy Tempest

In 1965, the Roy Tempest Organisation (RTO), of Nos 13-14 Dean Street in Soho, said they were the largest band agency in Europe. In their advertisement they listed many well-known bands, such as Georgie Fame, Zoot Money, The Moody Blues and Chris Farlowe, who had all appeared at Klooks Kleek, but not through Roy Tempest. There were also very popular groups such as The Yardbirds, The Pretty Things, Gene Vincent, none of whom ever played Klooks. In 1966 and 1967 Roy Tempest brought over several famous American groups, such as The Temptations and The Drifters, who toured Britain. But appearances were deceptive as one of the real group might be included, but often no-one was. It's hard to understand in this age of the internet that back in the 1960s, British fans who had bought the records, didn't really know what the singers looked like. They relied on photos in magazines or newspapers, but these were often poor quality. It seems Tempest imported unknown US groups who were then told they had to tour the UK under another name, such as 'The Original Drifters', and perform their famous songs.

As most of the groups were able to put on a good show, the fans went away happy. Even the clubs didn't realise they weren't getting the genuine article. Like many other promoters, Dick Jordan trusted Roy Tempest. The Drifters appeared at Klooks on 24 May 1966, and twice more in March and October 1967; The Temptations appeared on 5 September 1967 and then as The Fabulous Temptations on 5 December 1967.

However, things caught up with Roy Tempest on 21 November 1967, when Motown Records took him to court. He had brought over a group called The Velours who toured as The Fabulous Temptations. The judge ruled in favour of Motown Records and issued an order stopping RTO.

Looking back, Dick said:

> Roy Tempest's first forays into the American blues scene were I believe honest, although in retrospect I can't be 100 per cent certain that what I booked from him was initially the real thing: although Little Stevie Wonder and Freddie King were genuine. This is how it worked. Tempest would uncover some obscure American act and get them to rehearse The Drifters material. He'd then book them into reputable clubs, such as Klooks as; The 'ORIGINAL' Drifters. I and many other promoters fell for the scam simply because the 'ORIGINAL' appendage implied they were the 'original' band and not a covers version – which in fact they were – I even advertised them as The Drifters and dropped the 'original' tag.
>
> Tempest had offered me a reasonable price, explaining that if they could finish their spot at Klooks by 11 o'clock, a West End club would book them for a later second set, where the promoter would be told a similar story about Klooks. I was happy in my ignorance because I closed the club doors and made money. They weren't the only American 'original' band sold to me by Tempest, I also fell for the Fabulous Temptations.

According to a magazine article written by John Smith, entitled 'Fake Groups?' (*Soulful Kinda Music*, unknown date), The Velours had started in New York in 1956 and achieved several American hits but work dried up. They reformed in 1965 and were later brought over to England by Roy Tempest. After the court ruling they became known as The Fantastics who appeared at Klooks in June 1968 and again on 22 August 1968, booked through the reputable Harold Davison Agency. Smith said that Tempest also brought over a group called The Invitations, who performed as the Original Drifters.

Once the scam was exposed in the national press, bookings became more difficult and the RTO went into bankruptcy in March 1967. However, Roy started a new company at No. 76 Cavendish Street, but was again mentioned in bankruptcy proceedings in 1970 and 1972.

Eleanor Fleetham, archives researcher at the BBC, gave us the following information about Roy Tempest: he appeared on the BBC staff list in June 1973 as 'Sales and Marketing Manager' for Radio Enterprises, and by December 1973 he was listed under BBC Records Sales as 'Record Sales and Marketing Manager'. He last appeared on the BBC staff list in April 1977 and there is a handwritten note against his name stating that he left the BBC, presumably during that year.

George Melly

Klooks was getting good reviews in the press, and people such as George Melly particularly liked the club atmosphere. In the *Observer Weekend Review* for 28 February 1965, Melly wrote that over the last year the British version of R&B had elbowed the Liverpool groups, always excepting The Beatles, out of the charts. He talked about how British R&B had started in clubs like The Marquee and The Flamingo. He ended the article by saying:

> For people in London who would like to sample the music but feel nervous of Soho, I can recommend Klooks Kleek … The atmosphere is relaxed, the groups are drawn from both The Marquee and The Flamingo. The audience has the attentive gaiety that I remember in the early traditional jazz clubs at the beginning of the fifties.

Dick Jordan said that he and George Melly went back to the 'trad days': 'Whenever we met I usually bought him a double scotch as a thank you for his write ups of Klooks.'

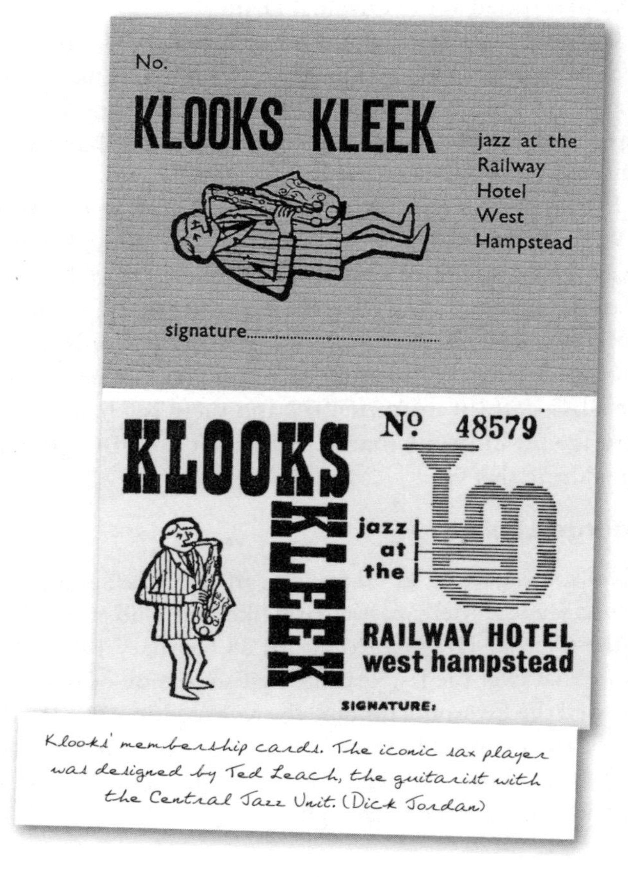

Klooks' membership cards. The iconic sax player was designed by Ted Leach, the guitarist with the Central Jazz Unit. (Dick Jordan)

YET MORE PERFORMERS

The names of the bands and musicians who appeared at Klooks reads like a list of 'Who's Who' in the music world.

Rod Stewart

'Rod the Mod', as he was known from his dress style, had played at Klooks in March 1965 with The Soul Agents when they supported American blues guitarist Buddy Guy. In May 1966 he joined the band The Shotgun Express. The line-up included Peter Green (guitar), Mick Fleetwood (drums), Peter Bardens (keyboards) and Dave Ambrose (bass). With Beryl Marsden and Rod, the band fronted two vocalists. The *Hampstead and Highgate Express* of 19 August 1966, reported:

> Klooks Kleek gave its floor space over to a new local group on Tuesday night called The Shotgun Express. Beryl Marsden, 18, was brought up in Liverpool. She jumped on stage while the Undertakers were performing and was invited to stay. She joined the Express in March. Rod Stewart has a style he calls 'Carnaby Street Soul'. He started as a tea boy in his brother's display firm, but went beatnik on the Continent. He slept in the Barcelona football stadium. He has appeared in the Hootchie Cootchie Men and the Soul Agents. ATV has run a feature around his egocentric mode of day-today living.

Rod joined with singers 'Long John' Baldry and Julie Driscoll, Brian Auger (organist), Richard Brown (bass), Vic Briggs (guitarist) and Mick Waller (drums), to form The Steampacket, a band which could potentially be called the first 'Supergroup'.

Denise Barrett worked at the coat check in Klooks. She started going to the Railway Hotel in Harrow, where she heard people like the Bo Street Runners, Long John Baldry and a weird band called the High Numbers, who later became more famous as The Who. She then discovered another Railway Hotel at West Hampstead:

> The first very impactful memory was a testosterone fuelled fight. Too much beer for the guys I guess. I remember Klooks was like a kind of first-floor ballroom, with a chandelier in the middle of the ceiling. When the fight broke out, the chandelier swung, some glasses were broken, but I don't think there were any casualties. The Steampacket played. Julie Driscoll, Rod Stewart; glam rock was born. I remember quite clearly that Rod had eye-wateringly tight pants and a cream satin frilled overshirt. And, he was wearing a necklace! A long string of crystal beads, and I remember thinking – he's got the beads from the drops of a chandelier!
>
> John Mayall's Bluesbreakers were a Klooks regular band. I met them when John McVie, Tom McGuiness, Peter Green and Hughie Flint were band members. I remember when a very shy, as yet to be stratospheric, amazing guitarist joined. Eric Clapton was a fixture at Klooks for a short time in my memory. I was great friends with John Mayall's drummer, Hughie Flint, and I travelled around London to see them play and hang out – to Bluesville at Manor House and the Rainbow at Finsbury Park.
>
> Another, surreal Klooks memory that has surfaced. At this time, I was a window dresser (art student substitute) at the flagship branch of Wallis (very groovy in those days), Marble Arch. I was a fashion bunny. Lots of velvet, lace, beads etc. And a very edgy coat. It was faux leather, maroon, fitted and double breasted with a little stand-up faux fur collar. But this coat, so feminine and shapely, had crinkles in its 'plastic' material. I walked into Klooks, very proud of my pretty purchase from Wallis, and Dick Jordan said: 'My god, she's wearing an elephant's foreskin coat!'

Cream

Cream were one of the most successful British Supergroups and played their own mix of blues and jazz. In 1966, Eric Clapton was playing with John Mayall's Bluesbreakers, Jack Bruce was in the Manfred Mann band and Ginger Baker was with the Graham Bond Organization (GBO). Because of Graham's drug problems and erratic behavior, Ginger was effectively running GBO and wanted to form his own group. He went to see Eric while he was playing at Oxford and discussed the idea. Eric responded positively and suggested Jack as the bass player. He was not fully aware that Jack and Ginger had previously had a huge row on stage while they were in the GBO and that Jack had walked out. Ginger wasn't so happy with the idea but he went to see Jack who agreed to form the new group. The three of them met at Ginger's house, No. 154 Braemar Avenue, in Neasden to rehearse. The first Cream gig was at Manchester's Twisted Wheel on 29 July 1966. Then on Sunday 31 July they played at the Windsor Jazz and Blues Festival. Although it poured with rain, Cream caused a sensation. Their manager, Robert Stigwood, thought they would have a similar appeal as the GBO and had booked them into a number of clubs on the blues circuit. Two days after their success at Windsor they played their first London gig at Klooks Kleek on 2 August.

Ginger Baker playing in the Graham Bond Organisation. (Dick Jordan)

Dick Jordan said:

> I received a phone call from Robert Masters, the booking agent for the Robert Stigwood Organisation, selling and extolling the virtues of a new three piece rock band, with NO saxophone OR Hammond organ! I could tell Robert was already aware of his task. But the band members were already well known to me and I was in no doubt about their potential and immediately agreed on a date for Cream.

Chris Welch of the *Melody Maker*, who saw the importance of Cream very early on and has written a book about them, heard the group play at Klooks:

> My strongest memory is of going to see Cream play there on 2 August 1966. It was a hot, sunny day, and I parked my black Ford Consul nearby, having driven all the way from Catford without fear of congestion charges or parking wardens. As I approached the rear door of the club, up the street wandering towards me were Jack Bruce and Ginger Baker, both smoking joints, which I was offered and helped create a receptive mood for the gig. I guess there must have been a queue of fans waiting for Cream but don't recall any hassle about getting in. No laminates or passes required – just show your face and walk in. I was however surprised, even then, by the supremely casual way the group assembled for what was after all an eagerly awaited gig by a heavily publicised (by me) gig. But then 'rock' was young, and only a small percentage of the population had any awareness of the importance of the music being created in such humble settings as Klooks Kleek. Soon Cream and bands like them would be playing Madison Square Garden and the Royal Albert Hall. For the moment the pop world centered upon an upstairs room in a London pub. 'Sorry mate – no crisps.'

> Cream were terrific at Klooks – Ginger pounding his drums, Jack wailing on harmonica, and the wonderful Eric of course, Mr Cool in his sideburns and with that calming sense of authority as soon as he played the guitar. The room was packed but I made sure I was in the front row, to catch sight of Ginger's epic drum solo in particular.

Geoff remembers Ginger asking him how much they were getting on their percentage deal for the evening, and expecting a grumpy response to the reply of £89. Instead, Ginger expressed surprise – bands he had been in at Klooks had usually been on about £50 – and thanks. Maybe he felt good because Cream were about to embark on their initial US tour playing stadia for five-figure dollar sums each night. A far cry from £89!

Cream's popularity grew very quickly and the only other time they played at Klooks was on 15 November. In the *Melody Maker* of 26 November 1966, Chris Welch reviewed Cream's gig at Klooks the previous week:

> Any doubts about the Cream's ability to perform as a group and not just three star soloists were dispelled by their sensational set at KK. In fact one of their main strengths proved to be the fantastic empathy that exists between them. Reports have been filtering in of bad performances by the Cream, but here they were seen to be obviously enjoying each other's playing tremendously, and working together like a team of bomb disposal experts. Eric Clapton played one of the most astonishing solos of his career on 'Steppin' Out', which he sustained for minutes on end. Ginger Baker battered fill-ins and off-beats with frightening ferocity, and Jack Bruce rivalled Eric's virtuosity with an incredible harmonica solo on 'Train Time' and 'Rolling and Tumbling'. Eric sang with feeling and Jack's bass playing was as fast and powerful as the Flying Scotsman. Here is one of the most musically rewarding groups making it today, and if anybody should record a 'live' LP it's the Cream.

Eric Clapton, 1975. (Matt Gibbons)

This gig was recorded live next door at Decca Studios, and Cream thought about releasing it as a four-track EP, but decided against it as EP sales had declined. They saw the LP as the way forward.

Fresh Cream, the group's first album, was released at the end of 1966. It reached Number 6 in the UK and Number 36 in the US charts. The following year they recorded *Disraeli Gears* in the US, which reached Number 5 in both charts. However, Cream would disband in July 1968 despite their many successes. In 2005 they briefly reunited for four shows in the Albert Hall and three in New York.

Jack Bruce had a local connection to West Hampstead. He was classically trained at the Royal Scottish Academy of Music but also played jazz and blues. In 1962, soon after he arrived in London, he shared a flat with trombonist John Mumford on the top floor of Alexandra Mansions on West End Green. On 26 September 1964, Jack married Janet Godfrey, who was the secretary of the Graham Bond fan club and who later helped with the lyrics of some of the Cream songs. They moved to a flat at No. 25 Bracknell Gardens, just off the Finchley Road, and not far from Jack's old home.

Elton John

On the 11 May 1967 a band called Bluesology played at Klooks. The keyboard player was called Reg Dwight, who in December 1967 combined the names of fellow band members Elton Dean and Long John Baldry to become Elton John. Previously, in July 1965, Bluesology had auditioned at The State Cinema in Kilburn and went professional with the Roy Tempest Organisation As most people know, Elton John went on to achieve considerable success.

Jimi Hendrix

The phenomenal American guitarist Jimi Hendix arrived in London on 24 September 1966 and spent some time sitting in with various bands. His manager Chas Chandler, previously the bass player with The Animals, saw Jimi playing in America and signed him up. In England, Chandler formed the three-piece Jimi Hendrix Experience with Noel Redding (bass) and Mitch Mitchell (drums), in October 1966. There are several references on the internet which say that Jimi Hendrix played at Klooks, but Dick and Geoff pointed out that they never booked him.

Dick later remembered:

> The first time Geoff and I witnessed Jimi Hendrix in action was at The Cromwellian, a music and drinking club in the Cromwell Road owned by 'Doctor Death', the wrestler. Zoot Money's band was playing and he casually invited Jimi to jam a few numbers with them. We couldn't believe our ears, it was like nothing we'd heard before and we wanted more. Knowing Chas Chandler, Jimi's manager, there was hope I'd receive an early booking to help fill his date sheet, but just a month or two later, Jimi's fee had gone ballistic and small clubs like Klooks were out priced.

Although never booked, Jimi did in fact appear at Klooks, dressed in red velvet trousers and a poncho at a time when Swinging London and psychedelia were in their infancy. His appearance alone caused looks and comments. On 17 October 1967, John Mayall and his band were playing one of their many gigs at West Hampstead. During the break the drummer Keef Hartley remembers talking to a young American guitarist in what passed as the Klooks dressing room. He recalls that 'he was so shy that he did not respond to me. His manager, Chas Chandler, was showing him round the British clubs.'

It was agreed that Jimi could sit in for the second set and borrow Mick Taylor's guitar. But when he picked it up he accidentally hit the low ceiling. Harry Bowles, one of the doormen, remembers that in the confusion Jimi's money fell out of his pockets onto the stage. But the minor mayhem didn't faze him. After checking there was no damage to the guitar, Jimi Hendrix played a blistering set holding the right-handed guitar upside down, as he was left handed. A short piece in the *Record Mirror* for 28 October confirms that Jimi sat in at Klooks and jammed with John Mayall. Hendrix and Mayall were part of the successful British blues tour of America in January 1968.

Fleetwood Mac

With their first gig on 19 September 1967, the original Fleetwood Mac played a total of six times at Klooks over the next two years, until their success in America transformed them into a stadium band. The band was formed in the summer of 1967 by guitarist Peter Green, Mick Fleetwood and John McVie, all of whom had played with John Mayall's Bluesbreakers. On vocals and guitar they had Jeremy Spencer. The band's name came from Peter Green naming a track on their recording session after the rhythm section of Mick Fleetwood (drums) and John McVie (bass). Despite having chart success from as early as Spring 1968, the band insisted on playing occasional gigs at Klook's.

Christine Perfect from Chicken Shack (keyboards and vocals), and John McVie's wife at the time, joined Fleetwood Mac in May 1969. In 1975, the band reformed in America with Lindsey Buckingham (guitar) and Stevie Nicks (vocals). Fleetwood Mac's platinum selling hit album *Rumours* was released in 1977. And since then the hits have kept on coming.

Led Zeppelin

On 1 April 1969, Led Zeppelin played their only gig at Klooks. A few days earlier they appeared at the National Jazz and Blues Festival at Richmond, where they attracted a huge audience and major press reaction. Brian Wilcock, who had been the DJ at Klooks for several years and was now the tour manager of Savoy Brown, suggested to Dick and Geoff that they advertise an April Fool spoof, 'Klooks Kleek National Festival', with Led Zeppelin playing, supported by Savoy Brown. Word of Zeppelin's stunning performance in Richmond had got out, and the queue of people trying to get into Klooks stretched for 300 yards around the block at West Hampstead. Geoff remembers the night well:

> It took the best part of an hour to persuade people to go once we were full. Those queuing on the stairs assumed they would get in when someone left, BUT who was going to leave before the group finished? We had the same but a lesser problem with some of the Georgie Fame nights. The Irish pub manager Pat Linnane, would be coming up every ten minutes saying, 'When are youse clearing this safety problem?'

Zeppelin guitarist Jimmy Page said:

> We loved doing gigs in places like Klooks Kleek, but in the end they were turning away more people than could actually see the show.

Brian Wilcock said that Savoy Brown also went down a storm, and that so many promoters turned up that night, that they got twenty-two new gigs from the show.

PUBLICITY

Klooks Kleek was well known for its unusual and humorous publicity material which tried to be edgy but easily recognisable. Thus the well-known breath-freshener advert of the time – 'Someone isn't using Amplex' – led to the eye-catching poster below. Unintentionally, the picture Dick had chosen for the 'someone not using' person looked very much like John Maule, who worked with Geoff in the front of house. For weeks afterwards he had people staring at him, and the ones who knew him well occasionally doing a quick sniff!

British society in the early years of Klooks was still fairly conservative; 'Beyond the Fringe' had been and gone, and 'That Was The Week That Was' was still to come. Dick and Geoff thought a bit of cheekiness would cause people to remember the club. It was almost schoolboyish compared to today's alternative comedy, but business cards reading 'BALLS!',

SOMEONE ISN'T USING

KLOOKS KLEEK

(Courtesy of Dick Jordan)

(Courtesy of Dick Jordan)

and in much smaller letters 'Every week at Klooks Kleek', had to be reprinted instantly because so many members wanted to show them to their friends. Similarly, the ultra-violet pass-out stamp on patrons' hands would say, for example, 'Sex', 'Knickers' or 'Bum', and cause hoots of laughter from those seeing them for the first time. These minor initiatives created a happy ambience and rapport with the members, who often commented that they felt the management set out to entertain them and make them feel part of the club, rather than just the customers listening to a group, as they were in other venues.

With Dick and Geoff both in day jobs and living in different parts of The Wood, conveniently situated pubs and even one of the benches outside St John's Wood tube station became their Jazz Contemporaries company 'office'. A leaflet declaring Klooks to be 'an oasis of happiness' was conceived and written on the bench, with Dick's girlfriend Birdy (and wife of forty-five years today) adding the finishing touches as she arrived back from work. In the early days when the club was struggling financially, Birdy, who ran the cloak room, gave Dick all the takings which helped Klooks to survive.

In 1967, Dick even created a mythical award to give Klooks some publicity:

> One piece of publicity that made an impact was 'The Carl Fischer Annual Awards'. Carl Fischer didn't exist, but once a year the celebrations would take place and award Klooks Kleek as the best club in the country, for two years running I might add. Our DJ, Pat B became the Best DJ in the country, an accolade that gave Pat more work than he could handle. We didn't push our luck too far, two awards in two years was sufficient enough for our members to feel proud they were members of an award-winning club and sadly Carl Fischer was killed off in a fishing tragedy.
>
> DJ Pat Boland worked for free providing that Klooks paid for something like three new records a week which he could use on his other gigs. It was a good deal for us because he chose records that people could dance to.

Geoff added:

> Pat Boland was a character. He looked like your average freak at the time, but he had his finger on the pulse when it came to good popular music. People even used to seek assurance that 'that DJ' was on duty.

THE INFAMOUS KLOOKS COACH TRIPS

Dick and Geoff wanted Klooks to be more than just a music venue, so they organised several activities to make it a real club for the members. A popular outing was the summer coach trip, which in 1965 went to Southsea. But things didn't go to plan that first year, as Geoff remembers:

Klooks coach trip, August 1967, with the 'sex club' poster in the rear window. (Dick Jordan).

> We had a problem identifying a pub which would accept coaches, but persuaded a grumpy landlord to open his function room after he'd made a mental calculation of the number of pints and gin and oranges in prospect. The beer was so awful we left without finishing a single pint. It was like a movie scene with people sidling out one by one. And I've never drunk a Gale's ale since, although my ale-drinking friends assure me that it was a 'nice drop' if well-kept.

Dick recalls that a second trip to Brighton in 1967 was more successful, although not for the reasons he hoped for:

> As soon as the coach had left the Railway Hotel and began its journey through London's traffic, remember no M25 then, we'd stop at a traffic light and the odd motorist or two who'd been following the coach would impatiently tap on the coach door requesting membership forms for

Klooks Kleek. We'd taped a signature poster on the back window of the coach and assumed they were rock fans interested in Klooks and how effective our worldwide advertising was proving! But no, the poster they'd been interested in was another joke one we'd pasted up for 'Klooks Kleek Sex Club', and this was the club grabbing their attention.

DOPEY DICK'S JAZZ CLUB

On 5 April 1967, after a gap of two and a half years, Dick thought the time was right to try and reintroduce a regular jazz night. But this time he used a different approach. With the help of Ronnie Scott and his business partner Pete King, visiting American jazz artists who were booked to play at Ronnie's Frith Street Club also played a set at Dopey's. The revival was short-lived, but while it lasted the audiences enjoyed performances from a number of leading jazz musicians. As Dick explained:

> In 1967, jazz was certainly making a minor comeback in London. Ronnie Scott's was attracting larger audiences and I felt it the right time to open a modern jazz night at Klooks Kleek. It would be separate from Klooks, which was identified as a rock and blues club and because a small number of friends, including Geoff, said that I was crazy to get involved in jazz again, I decided to call the club 'Dopey Dick's'.
>
> Opening with Eddie Lockjaw Davis, the following weeks featured a wide range of British and American artists such as Roland Kirk, Sonny Rollins, Zoot Sims, Ben Webster, Yusef Lateef and Jimmy McGriff who I thought might attract some Georgie Fame fans, but no, we still lost money. The British held their own with the full The Ted

Heath Orchestra, minus the deceased Ted Heath unfortunately, and then conducted by Ralph Dolomore; Ronnie Scott, Kenny Graham's Afro Cubans and Tubby Hayes. Vocalists weren't forgotten either with Annie Ross, Mark Murphy, Dakota Staton and Blossom Dearie all making their inimitable impressions. Financially I wasn't doing as well as I'd hoped, especially with expensive Americans artistes and I thought the reason could be because so many of them had already spent two weeks beforehand at Ronnie's and could have been seen there. I mentioned this to Ronnie's business partner, Pete King, who understood my predicament and magnanimously suggested that the debut of their next American artist would be at Dopey Dick's. Keeping his word, Pete phoned later and offered me Coleman Hawkins and we confirmed dates. Unfortunately, the date would be the last night for Dopey Dick's, but what a way to go out!

Coleman Hawkins was getting on in years and not in the best of health. He hadn't played Britain for many years and the club was packed with eager punters and its full quota of jazz reviewers from most of the nationals and trade papers. The atmosphere in the room was something I'd never experienced before and Coleman re-enforced my belief that he was one of the most original tenor saxophonists of all time. There was an atmosphere of pure joy as Coleman played through his repertoire and one could feel how much he enjoyed it. He approached me at the end of the evening and rated the gig as one of the best he'd ever played. I didn't know whether to believe him or not and because it was the last night for Dopeys I wasn't sure if that was a good way to go out or not.

After Coleman's first number, Jack Bruce, playing on string bass in Coleman's backing group, complained that he couldn't hear himself play. Generally, backing groups provided their own sound equipment, but this being a

> jazz gig it was down to the promoter. Our rarely used but powerful ex-government amplifier had the bass turned down to zero. I turned it up to the top and immediately Jack's powerful bass and the rhythm section came alive and so did the rest of the band. If Jack hadn't complained who knows how Coleman Hawkins would have been received.

As a coda to the story, Dick was in New York two years later when he was managing an English band called Juniors Eyes. A&M Records were about to release the band's album and had provided a limo to take Dick to hear some music in Harlem and have a meal. Benny, the driver of the limo, kept looking at Dick:

> Benny kept staring at me through the mirror and said he'd met me before somewhere, but how could he when this was my first trip to New York. 'I don't forget a face man, I know we've met before, I just know it.' Then Benny said, 'I know where we met man, didn't you run a club in London?' It transpired that Benny had been the personal tour manager to Coleman Hawkins for many years and that Coleman had just died. 'I remember you man, you ran this club in Hampstead with all those stairs, Coleman was so out of breath when he'd climbed them that he was refusing to do the gig. He was so worried he wouldn't get his breath back to play his horn, but he did, I talked him in to it.' Benny told me later as we were returning to the hotel that Coleman had said it was one of his best gigs - ever!' So it confirmed that Coleman wasn't shooting me a line.

The new jazz club received very good reviews in the music press. For example, reporter Christopher Bird wrote in the *Melody Maker* of 29 April 1967:

There was no doubt at all that Ben Webster was firing on all cylinders in front of a large and enthusiastic crowd at Dopey Dick's' last Wednesday. So we've heard all the tunes before ... but like the man said, 'taint what you do etc' and the way that he did it was superb. All in all a great night, good to see Klooks back on the jazz map.

Yusef Lateef

Dick Weindling remembers hearing Yusef Lateef at Klooks on 9 August 1967. Yusef, born William Emanuel Huddleston, changed his name when he converted to the Muslim faith in 1950. August 1967 was a very hot summer night and Klooks was packed to see the tenor sax player. He was a large man with a shaved head, wearing a shiny American suit. The crowd was very enthusiastic, but when he played a strange wooden instrument which sounded a little like a Swannee whistle,

DOPEY DICKS jazzhouse
Railway Hotel, West Hampstead
Every Wednesday 8.00 - 11.00

APRIL 5th 10/-	Ex-Basie Sideman EDDIE 'Lockjaw' DAVIS Harold McNair Quartet
APRIL 12th 10/-	BUCK CLAYTON Johnny Chilton's Rhythm Kings Bob Stuckey Organ Quartet
APRIL 19th 10/-	BEN WEBSTER Pat Smythe Trio
APRIL 26th 15/-	SONNY ROLLINS Stan Tracey Trio Bob Stuckey Quartet
MAY 3rd 7/6	ALAN HAVEN/TONY CROMBIE DUO
MAY 10th 7/6	MARK MURPHY Jerry Allan Trio

Dopey Dick's leaflet, 1967.

KNOBLERS & KLACKERS
SLOOPS SLEEP
KLOCLES & KLETCHUP
KNOOZE KNEEZE
CLOOCS CLEEC
NO! NO! IT'S
~~KLEEKS KLOOK~~
SORRY
KLOOKS KLEEK
RAILWAY HOTEL WEST HAMPSTEAD
TUESDAYS 'N' THURSDAYS
RHYTHM 'N' BLUESDAYS
DOPEY DICKS jazzhouse
WEDNESDAYS MODERN JAZZ

Klooks and Dopey Dick's advert 1967 for the National Jazz and Blues Festival, 1967. (National Jazz and Blues Festival) (Dick Jordan)

they gasped. Yusef stopped playing thinking people didn't like it. At this point, noticing the worried look on his face, the crown cheered and with a huge smile, he continued playing to tremendous applause.

Ronnie Scott

Ronnie Scott and his quartet played at Dopey Dick's on 11 October 1967. Ronnie had helped Dick over the years and on this occasion the attendance was low. Blaming himself, Ronnie graciously refused to take any fee and offered to pay the band himself. As Dick said, 'What a gentleman.' Ronnie was an outstanding tenor player who opened his London club in 1959 in Gerrard Street. It moved to its present site in Frith Street in 1965. He was well known for his humorous introductions at the club, one of which he must have used a hundred times when someone was late or missing. With apologies to residents of a splendid town, 'He's been held up at a gig in Baldock' always brought the house down. In 1981, when he was awarded an OBE under his real name of Ronald Schatt, he was living in Messina Avenue, off West End Lane.

Dick talked about the house pianist, Colin Purbrook:

> At Dopey Dick's instead of booking an interval band we used instead a local jazz pianist from Fawley Road, Colin Purbrook. A solo pianist of exceptional style and originality, he was versatile enough to play bass in the Dudley Moore Trio. Visiting American musicians requested his services such as Chet Baker, Zoot Sims, Dexter Gordon and also Judy Garland. At Dopey's he was more than just a cocktail pianist and charmed his way with our audience. It was a joy to see him playing without being talked over. In later years he was resident at the L'Escargot and Kettner's Restaurants and he died in 1999 aged 66.

Unfortunately the interest in jazz just wasn't strong enough to sustain Dopey Dick's and on 24 November 1967, after running for eight months, the club closed. As Dick told the *Evening Standard* on 17 November:

> We've had all the best American players, but I can't make it pay. I've lost £1,250 since April. This week we had Roland Kirk and I still lost £100. I've advertised. I've handed out leaflets. I can't afford it any more. The jazz club has been subsidised by the R&B nights, but it can't go on. A top American jazz group costs £300 for the night and even charging £1 a time, I can't make ends meet.

Geoff later pointed out that the loss of £1,250 was a considerable amount of money in 1967. In comparison of the cost of the £300 a night fee, he said that his mortgage on a house in Sittingbourne, Kent, was £330 a year!

Miles Copeland

Towards the end of 1969, Dick met Miles Copeland, who later became the manager of The Police – his younger brother Stuart was the drummer:

> One night an American approached me at the club enquiring about securing an interval spot for a band he was managing. Sporting a short military style haircut and dressed in a single-breasted blazer with a college tie he looked the typical Ivy League scholar. His name was Miles Copeland. I recognised the name and asked whether he was related to the Miles Copeland I read about who had been an O.S.S. operative in World War Two and a founder member of the C.I.A. 'That's my father,' replied Miles. I liked Miles' approach, he possessed an air of confidence and knowing nothing of the band I knew they would be good. For some interval bands I offered nothing, but for

Miles's band I offered £5 which was a good fee. The band was Wishbone Ash and two years later in 1971 I would become their agent and work with Miles Copeland. I felt sure that one day he was destined to become a millionaire and I told him so. Miles laughed at my confidence but in 1977 when he became the manager of The Police, the millionaire tag I had bestowed upon him became a reality. In the meantime was going insane with the music business and left to recover my senses, my wife and two kids.

THE END OF KLOOKS

Towards the end of 1969, Dick had an offer to work on a feature film and he thought about making a major change in his life:

In the late Autumn of 1969 when more and more cinemas were closing down and putting Presburys' bread and butter on the line, I felt my job was becoming tenuous and wouldn't last much longer. John Brason, a film producer I'd known for many years, conveniently offered me a job as camera assistant on a six months feature film in Malta. With alternate weekend return flights back to London, all paid and with the benefit of above union rates, the timing was perfect.

Klooks was in its final death throes and would probably close within months. The film would give me the opportunity of putting money in the bank before deciding on what the next chapter of my life would be. So after eleven years at Presburys I handed in my notice and looked forward to flying out to Malta in January, the month that Klooks would close. The timings were so perfect that I believed fate was playing an important role in my future. But then on Christmas Eve 1969, John Brason phoned to say that the finance had been pulled on the picture and it was cancelled indefinitely. I was now out of work and a Merry Christmas was had by all!

The final nail in Klooks' coffin had nothing to do with financial losses. In December 1969, Watneys Brewery, who owned the Railway Hotel, told Dick and Geoff that it was to become the Birds Nest Disco, one of a chain they were opening in their pubs around London. Klooks could no longer use the pub.

There were more setbacks. Dick was still involved with the band Juniors Eyes when, in January 1970, the drummer John Cambridge announced he was leaving the group. The band had played on *Space Oddity* and become close to David Bowie, who offered John a job with his band, and that was the end of Juniors Eyes.

Keef Hartley and Samson, whose drummer later joined Iron Maiden, played the last session at Klooks on 28 January 1970.

The *Melody Maker* for 7 February 1970 carried a piece about the closure of Klooks Kleek. In an interview with Dick, the renowned music critic Max Jones (and Dick's next-door neighbour) said:

> Klooks Kleek closed last Wednesday night. Chicken Shack's guitarist Stan Webb and manager Harry Simmonds paid tribute to Dick Jordan. As he surveyed the large crowd, Dick joked, he would like to close again next Wednesday. He said he survived for so long (nine years), because of the agents and managers who have helped with the bookings. 'They enabled me to stay afloat.' He thought the time for small London clubs, and perhaps other cities, was almost up. One reason is the four new 'clubs' which are sufficient for the whole of London – the Royal Albert Hall, the Festival Hall, Lyceum and the Roundhouse.
>
> Four or five years ago music was split into two categories: pop and R&B. Now the picture is quite different, there is pop, blues, progressive rock, folk, soul, rock and roll, and reggae. Each section draws its own crowd so a promoter's potential audience is split into seven. We gave

> out 2,000 free tickets and only had 110 returned – in other words you can't give tickets away. When he started with jazz they had no bouncers. With R&B he took on six bouncers. 'From the day we booked the Cream, I noticed a difference. The crowd's attitude was more serious. That seriousness and devotion has increased so that loyalties have moved from the club to the band.'

Geoff later reflected on Klooks' demise:

> The names built up by people at Klooks Kleek and other clubs enabled them to go to much bigger venues for much bigger money. Georgie Fame had already established his name at The Flamingo Club, but Klooks introduced him to a different type of audience. He loved playing at KK, and his agents, the Gunnells, did do us a favour for a good year after his first chart hit by letting him do Klooks occasionally.
>
> But there was also an external element. From late 1967 onwards, the 'Swinging London' stuff had the US thirsting for British blues bands and as you've heard me say before, 'The next gig for X band would be a $50,000 one in a US stadium.' Finally, so-called psychedelic and prog-rock bands were gaining popularity, and that meant light shows and other emerging media. Klooks could accommodate a limited light show but not the large rigs that were coming into use. And if it had been possible to accommodate them, the rest of West Hampstead would have had to stay dark for the night!

Although he continued to work at the club on Tuesday nights, Geoff had decided, not long after moving to mid-Kent in 1966, that his long-term interest in international development and a desire to live and work overseas, took precedence over his involvement in the club. So, after Klook's closed for the last time, Geoff visited forty developing countries, lived with his family in two of them (Bangladesh and Tanzania) and on retirement in 1998 was awarded an OBE. Looking back, Geoff said:

> Such awards get a bland description, typically 'for services to (name your subject or institution)' and the recipient does not see the citation. So I don't know if it's for cheating death by poisoning (possibly intentional) in Bangladesh, when a tin of pineapple chunks and a persistent driver who woke me out of a semi-coma at every ferry point and forced me to re-hydrate on coconut water managed to get me home and not in a box. Probably not, because only a couple of people were aware of the incident. It might have been for surviving gunpoint arrest in Africa over a misunderstanding on vehicle licensing, but again probably not because only two or three people know about it. Or it could have been for dedication to the job and tending to the needs of fastidious senior people in my final overly-long job in personnel. What's the bet?

After he retired from the civil service Geoff did freelance work, which included living with volcanic ash in Montserrat, and in Kabul listening to rockets land at the end of the road and 'little' IEDS going pop-pop round the boundary wall of the house. They were letting them know that they knew where they lived. That's what one might be awarded an OBE for, but Geoff already had one!

Geoff Williams, 1968, by Hartley.

After Klooks closed, Dick had a call from the BBC's *Late Night Line Up* programme. Someone who worked on the show had been a club member of Klooks. They wanted to film the story and asked Dick to set up the stage, the spots, and the ubiquitous gingham tablecloths and to put up a collection of 'Coming Soon' posters. They filmed there on 19 February 1970, but Dick said he was low and depressed about seeing Klooks lit up again but empty, not just of the crowds, but no Geoff, no John or Harry, and a silent stage and his future in abeyance. The piece was shown later that month.

Incredibly, when it finally shut its doors in January 1970, Klooks Kleek had reached a total of 58,000 members!

KLOOKS AT THE LYCEUM

After the closure of the club at the Railway Hotel and Dick's abortive film job in Malta, he was offered a job with Marquee Martin, an agency booking a large number of bands, including Black Sabbath, Yes, The Strawbs, and Taste, among others. In the summer of 1970, Klooks had one last incarnation as 'Klooks at the Lyceum'. Big name bands were booked by the Marquee Martin agency for a series of Friday night gigs. These were held at the famous Lyceum Theatre and ballroom in London's West End, beginning on 17 July and lasting for the summer.

Dick recalls that Rod Stewart particularly remembered one of these gigs:

> On 18 September we booked the Kinks, supported by the Faces with Rod Stewart. There was a bet in the agency that the Kinks would pull out at the eleventh hour, and they did. The Faces agency were offered top of the bill and an hour before opening there was a queue round the Lyceum. The waiting crowd were informed that the Kinks had cancelled and the Faces would now be head lining.

Klooks at the Lyceum, with Black Sabbath. (Dick Jordan)

> Summertime London was full of American tourists experiencing Swinging London and it appeared most of them were in the queue to see Rod Stewart. I expected much of the crowd to disperse, but they didn't. The Lyceum was packed to capacity and the Faces produced one of the best nights we'd had with the press agreeing and giving rave reviews. Rod often told me the Lyceum gig triggered off an upturn in his career.

In May 1971, Dick left Marquee Martin to join Miles Copeland and John Sherry's agency, where he continued to book big name bands such as Queen, The Police, Jeff Beck and The Average White Band. He later worked for the artist agency Folio before he retired to Wales.

Many people who went to Klooks in the 1960s still have fond memories, as these quotes written on a website called 'Down the Lane' in 2010 show:

> I couldn't wait to buy Friday's *Melody Maker* to find out who was playing there.
>
> Without a doubt Klooks Kleek was the best live venue to catch anyone who was going to be anyone or already was!

Klooks at the Lyceum, Kinks. (Dick Jordan)

To illustrate the point that people still remember Klooks, Dick said:

> A few years ago, my sister who worked at Klooks and who now lives near West End Lane, was approached by a smart-looking gentleman on West End Green. He asked her politely if she remembered Klooks Kleek? It turned out that he had been one of our bouncers and remembered her after forty years.

THE MOONLIGHT AND STARLIGHT CLUBS

After Klooks closed in January 1970 there was a gap of several years before live music started again at the Railway Hotel. The first adverts for bands in the *NME Gig Guide* are shown as 'The Railway Hotel, West Hampstead', for 9 January 1978. Then, on 6 October 1979, the name the Moonlight Club is used. This was run by the promoter Dave Kitson, and guitarist Andrew Wyatt, who lived in West Hampstead, operated the sound system. Seeing the success of the club, the pub manager open a second club called The Starlight upstairs in the large room on the first floor previously used by Klooks. The Starlight and Moonlight Clubs were run at the same time for a few years. This continued until 29 October 1993 when the clubs closed for good.

The bands appearing reflected the changing style of music, but some of the more famous included: Squeeze, 12 December 1977; Adam Ant and the Antz played there a number of time between April and December 1978; The Cure in 1978; and The Damned were there on 30 April 1979. The Specials played in May 1979 and a bootleg recording appeared as *The Specials Live At The Moonlight Club.*

A new Camden Town band played at the Moonlight on 3 July 1979, just two months after they first appeared as Madness. On their first tour outside Ireland, U2 played at the Moonlight on 1 December 1979. The Manchester band Joy Division, were there on 4 April 1980, and Depeche Mode were there in 1981. The Stone Roses played on 23 October 1984. That night, Pete Townsend jammed with the Stone Roses playing The Who songs 'Substitute' and 'The Kids are Alright'.

Dick Jordan at the Railway, 2013.

In October 1979, the Moonlight was also home to 6Ts Soul Nites, when records were played by a DJ. The 6Ts club was the brainchild of two soul fanatics, Ady Croasdell and Randy Cozens, and it stayed at the Railway for fifteen months before moving to Oxford Street.

Zoot and Geoff Williams, 2013.

On 21 March 2013 to celebrate the writing of this book, Dick Jordan, Geoff Williams and Zoot Money met up for a reunion at the Railway Hotel, where they were interviewed by the *Hampstead and Highgate Express*.

APPENDIX

THE BANDS WHO PLAYED AT KLOOKS KLEEK AND DOPEY DICK'S

Complied by Geoff Williams from the original bookings records. The numbers in brackets show the total appearances. The bands are divided into the top billing and interval bands. The comments are by Geoff Williams.

Top Billing of Blues, R&B and Rock Artists

Name of Band	Appearance Dates (Tuesdays unless marked Monday⁺, or Thursday*)
Aardvark	09/12/69
Alan Bown Set/ The Alan Bown! (8)	08/09/66*, 09/02/67*, 06/06/67, 5/07/67, 31/10/67, 20/02/68, 13/08/68, 16/12/69 1969 singer Robert Palmer topped '80s pop charts with 'Addicted to Love'

The Alan Price Set (2)	22/03/66, 07/03/67 Alan was the singer and keyboardist in The Animals where he was succeeded by Dave Rowberry of the Mike Cotton Sound. Later had chart hits both solo and duetting with Georgie Fame
The Alex Harvey Band (11)	07/04/64, 02/06/64, 07/07/64, 12/01/65, 23/02/65, 04/05/65, 01/06/65, 02/11/65, 14/12/65, 04/01/66, 29/03/66 Billed as The Sensational AHB and they certainly gave it everything. Brother Les joined Stone the Crows and, sadly, was electrocuted on stage during a concert
Alexis Korner (5)	12/05/64, 15/06/64⁺, 08/09/64, 29/12/64, 20/04/65 R&B veteran who, in his 40s, finally had hits with '70s band CCS, including 'Whole Lotta Love', a cover of a Led Zeppelin song, used as the *Top of the Pops* theme
Alvin Cash	17/01/67
Amboy Dukes (17)	17/11/66★, 19/01/67★, 16/03/67★, 04/05/67★, 20/07/67★, 24/08/67★, 29/02/68★, 18/04/68★, 06/06/68★, 15/08/68★, 12/09/68★, 24/10/68★, 28/11/68★, 16/01/69★, 06/03/69★, 17/04/69★, 31/07/69★ Creation of two former John Mayall sidemen. Not to be confused with US group of the same name

Artwoods (9)	22/06/64+, 20/07/64+, 03/08/64+, 14/09/64+, 01/12/64, 19/01/65, 13/04/65, 29/06/65, 04/10/65 Ronnie Wood's big brother's band, also billed as the Art Woods Combo, graduated from interval gigs and was an early KK fixture. Included Jon Lord, future star with Deep Purple
Arthur Brown (Crazy World of)	29/08/67 Introduced a circus element to festivals by being lowered to the stage by crane wearing a flaming crown. Solid rocking sound
Atomic Rooster	30/09/69 Two single hits, lots of festivals and US work up to '74
Aynsley Dunbar Retaliation (6)	28/11/67, 30/01/68, 19/03/68, 20/08/68, 29/10/68, 07/10/69 Former Mayall drummer's group played **very last Tuesday gig at Klook's Kleek, 27/01/70**
Ben E. King	22/11/66 Hit-maker with The Drifters and as a solo singer
Billy Woods	07/10/65*
Blackcat Bones	14/01/69
Blodwyn Pig	05/08/69
Blossom Toes (2)	15/04/69, 12/08/69
Bluesology	11/05/67* One of the members of this group now goes by the name of Sir Elton Hercules John
Bo Diddley	18/04/67 with The Canadians
Bo Street Runners	03/11/64

Brian Auger Trinity (10)	22/03/65[+], 15/04/65★, 13/06/65 with Jimmy James, 12/10/65, 25/10/66, 28/05/68, 02/09/69, 10/08/69★, 12/10/69★, 07/12/69★ Brian played both modern jazz and R&B gigs at KK, with his own group, as a member of The Steampacket and as a duo with Julie Driscoll
Buddy Guy	01/03/65[+] with Rod Stewart's Soul Agents. Yes, him!
Carl Douglas (7)	02/03/67★, 13/04/67★, 13/07/67★, 09/11/67★, 14/12/67★, 28/03/68★, 11/04/68★
Cat's Pyjamas	28/12/67★
Champion Jack Dupree	25/05/65 with John Mayall's Bluesbreakers
The Chants	07/12/65
Charlesworth Big Blues	04/05/64[+]
Chessmen (5)	16/11/64[+], 16/02/65, 06/03/65, 15/06/65, 27/07/65
The Chiffons	13/06/66
Chicken Shack (4)	03/09/68, 11/02/69, 25/03/69, 23/09/69 Singer Christine Perfect was married to John Mayall bassist John McVie and followed him into Fleetwood Mac and their lucrative US incarnation
Chris Farlowe and the Thunderbirds (15)	22/04/64★, 25/05/64[+], 29/06/64[+], 04/08/64, 06/10/64, 09/11/64[+], 15/12/64, 16/03/65, 11/05/65, 1/07/65★, 16/09/65★, 14/10/65★, 08/03/66, 17/05/66, 11/07/67 The guitarist in the Thunderbirds was Albert Lee, who would later feature in Heads, Hands & Feet, and with Clapton, The Crickets, Emmylou etc. The 'guitarists' guitarist

Cliff Bennett and the Rebel Rousers (5)	11/10/66, 16/05/67, 07/11/67, 26/09/68★, 13/02/69★. Final gig backed by The Cliff Bennett Band, having parted with The Rebel Rousers
Clouds	30/10/69★
The Counts (2)	09/07/68, 17/10/68★
The Cream (2)	02/08/66, 15/11/66 Baker, Bruce and Clapton formed the first of the Supergroups
Dave Antony's Moods (7)	02/12/65★, 16/06/66★, 18/08/66★, 06/10/66★, 27/07/66, 27/10/66★, 01/12/66★
Dave Davani (3)	11/05/64+, 30/06/64, 22/09/64
Dedicated Men	12/08/65★
Dee Dee Warwick	31/10/68★ with The Impressions
Deep Purple	26/08/69 Hit the big time one year later
The Drifters (3)	24/05/66 with The League of Gentlemen, 21/03/67 with The Canadians, 24/10/67 with The Garden of Eden
East of Eden	02/10/69
Eclection	28/01/69
Eddie Boyd	13/02/68 with Chicken Shack
Eddie Thornton	10/07/69
Edwin Starr	07/02/67 Motown artist already with minor hits
Eire Apparent	03/12/69
Fabulous Temptations	05/09/67 billed as The Temptations, 05/12/67
Family (7)	16/04/68, 23/07/68, 08/10/68, 19/11/68, 04/03/69, 15/07/69, 14/10/69 Last gig immediately pre-dated first chart hit of popular '70s band
Fantastics (2)	11/06/68, 22/08/68★
Felders Orioles (2)	09/06/66★, 27/04/67★

The Fenmen	10/01/67
Ferris Wheel (11)	22/08/67, 19/12/67, 08/02/68★, 14/03/68★, 25/04/68★, 30/05/68★, 25/07/68★ 10/10/68★, 05/12/68★, 02/01/69★, 20/02/69★
Fleetwood Mac (6)	19/09/67, 14/11/67, 06/02/68, 02/04/68, 17/09/68, 18/11/69 The original band formed by Peter Green, Mick Fleetwood and John McVie, all from Mayall's Bluesbreakers. Chart hits began in Spring '68, but the band insisted on playing occasional gigs at Klooks. Christine Perfect would join in 1970 followed by US artistes Lindsey Buckingham and Stevie Nicks and enormous success
Freddie King (2)	25/02/69, 10/06/69 with Killing Floor
Garnet Mimms	01/05/69★
The Gass (10)	10/03/66★, 22/06/67★, 03/08/67★, 02/11/67★, 21/12/67★, 22/02/68★, 11/04/68★ backing Carl Douglas, 13/06/68★, 18/07/68★, 21/11/68★
Georgie Fame/ Georgie Fame's Band (22)	10/09/63 **Opening Tuesday R&B**, 08/10/63, 22/10/63, 05/11/63, 26/11/63, 10/12/63, 24/12/63, 07/01/64, 21/01/64, 11/02/64, 25/02/64, 31/03/64, 13/04/64[+] **First Monday session**, 19/05/64, 08/06/64[+], 14/07/64, 02/11/64[+], 21/09/64[+], 04/01/65[+], 26/07/65[+] **Last Monday**, 23/11/65, 27/10/65 (band only) The legend. He gave Klooks Kleek impetus
Girl Talk	26/06/69

Graham Bond (39)	17/09/63, 01/10/63, 29/10/63, 19/11/63, 17/12/63 with Duffy Power, 14/01/64, 28/01/64, 18/02/64, 10/03/64, 24/03/64, 21/04/64, 27/04/64⁺, 18/05/64⁺, 09/06/64, 23/06/64, 27/07/64⁺, 18/08/64, 01/09/64, 05/10/64⁺, 26/10/64⁺, 8/12/64, 22/02/65⁺, 08/04/65*, 20/05/65*, 22/06/65, 17/08/65, 21/09/65, 16/11/65, 23/12/65*, 25/01/65, 01/03/66, 05/04/66, 28/06/66, 08/11/66, 28/02/66, 08/07/67, 12/12/67, 04/11/69, 23/12/69 Another legend. Played Klooks as a jazz musician and R&B group. The 1963–66 band included Jack Bruce, Ginger Baker (both later in Cream), John McLaughlin (Mahavishnu Orchestra etc.), West Hampstead resident Dick Heckstall-Smith (Mayall, Colosseum, solo jazz artiste), but never had a hit. Twice recorded at KK; by Giorgio Gomelsky and KK bouncer Ray Goganian, tapes believed lost but re-emerged in 2009
Greatest Show on Earth	27/02/69*
Gypsy	16/10/69*
Happy Magazine (2)	01/08/68* 19/09/68*
Hardin & York	20/01/70 Ex Spencer Davis duo who formed just in time to play KK!
Hard Meat (2)	19/08/69, 14/01/70 - Weds
Herbie Goins (3)	23/03/65 with The Night-Timers, 14/02/67, 04/07/67
Howlin' Wolf & Hubert Sumlin (2)	14/12/64⁺, 27/05/69 backed by John Dummer
Interstate Roadshow	09/01/69*
Jackie Edwards	05/05/66*

Jethro Tull (2)	18/06/68, 05/11/68 Another to go on to mega-hits in USA
Jimmy Cliff (4)	17/02/66★, 24/03/66★, 21/07/66★, 20/06/68★
Jimmy James (8)	13/07/65 with the Brian Auger Trinity, 09/09/65★, 23/08/66, 29/11/66, 04/04/67, 20/06/67, 15/08/67, 30/04/68
Jimmy Nicol	13/10/64 Had made a name as Ringo's stand-in when the Beatle was ill, but did not crack the R&B market with this group
John L Watson (3)	09/03/67★, 18/05/67★, 29/06/67★ with The Web
John Lee Hooker (3)	12/10/64+ with John Lee's Groundhogs, 13/05/65★ with Cops 'n' Robbers, 27/06/67 with Savoy Brown
John Mayall (33)	13/07/64+, 11/08/64, 24/08/64+, 07/09/64+, 29/09/64, 17/11/64, 07/12/64+ **'John Mayall plays John Mayall Live at Klooks Kleek!'** 28/12/64+, 01/02/65+, 30/03/65, 10/06/65★, 08/07/65★, 29/07/65★, 24/08/65, 30/09/65★, 26/10/65, 11/11/65★, 28/12/65, 08/02/66, 10/05/66, 05/07/66, 20/09/66, 13/12/66, 14/03/67 with Eddie Boyd, 23/05/67, 08/08/67, 17/10/67, 02/01/68, 05/03/68, 07/05/68, 02/07/68, 21/01/69, 01/07/69 Employed and sacked many of the star names of the era. No chart success in UK, but enormous concert, festival, album success after moving to USA

Jon Hiseman's Colosseum (3)	22/10/68, 04/02/69, 11/03/69 Another former sideman in a John Mayall band who formed the very successful Colosseum who are still performing
José Feliciano	01/06/67★ with Rosco Brown
Joyce Bond (3)	19/12/68★, 10/04/69★, 03/07/69★
Juicy Lucy	30/12/69
Julian Covey	30/05/67
Julie Driscoll	17/12/68 with Brian Auger (*see* The Steampacket)
Junior's Eyes (8)	15/10/68, 12/11/68, 07/01/69, 18/03/69, 06/05/69, 09/09/69, 25/09/69★, 28/10/69
Keef Hartley (4)	26/11/68, 13/05/69, 21/10/69 Yet another Mayall sideman to form a group which would also play **28/01/70, a Wednesday, and the last-ever night of Klook's Kleek.**
Keith Relf's Renaissance (2)	22/07/69, 02/12/69 Former Yardbird who moved on as they moved to pop
Led Zeppelin	01/04/69 Jimmy Page, ex Yardbird, was the only 'name' in a group which would break album sales records within a year – and broke the record for the most people turned away from a bursting Klooks!
Lee Dorsey	03/05/66 with The League of Gentlemen
Lee Hawkins (2)	08/05/69★, 07/08/69★
Little Walter	28/09/64+ with The Sheffields
Liverpool Scene (2)	08/04/69, 03/06/69
Long John Baldry (5)	02/02/65, 10/08/65 with The Steampacket, 31/01/67, 02/05/67, 12/09/67
Lou Johnson	14/09/65 with the Sonny Childe Cool School
Lowell Fulsom	20/05/69 with Steve Miller

Mae Mercer	08/02/65⁺ with Artwoods
Marmalade	26/03/68
Max Baer	07/09/67★
Maxine Brown	26/09/67 with Q Set
Memphis Slim	25/08/65 with The Sheffields
Mighty Baby (3)	24/07/69, 23/10/69★, 21/01/70 - Weds
Mike Cotton Sound (45)	18/01/65⁺, 15/03/65⁺, 29/04/65★, 17/06/65★,2 0/07/65, 23/09/65★, 03/04/66★, 31/03/66★, 07/04/66★, 21/04/66★, 28/04/66★, 12/05/66★, 19/05/66★, 02/06/66★, 23/06/66★, 30/06/66★, 07/07/66★, 14/07/66★, 04/08/66★, 11/08/66★, 25/08/66★, 01/09/66★, 22/09/66★, 29/09/66★, 13/10/66★, 20/10/66★, 03/11/66★, 10/11/66★, 24/11/66★, 08/12/66★, 22/12/66★, 05/01/67★, 12/01/67★, 16/02/67★, 30/03/67★, 20/04/67★, 25/05/67★, 01/08/67, 10/10/67, 16/11/67★, 01/02/68★, 23/05/68★, 05/09/68★, 24/04/69★,15/05/69★. Former trad jazz trumpeter who embraced amplified sound. Became the 'house band' for Klooks Thursdays. Very popular, they played more gigs than any other band
Misunderstood	29/07/69
Mose Allison	24/08/64⁺
The Nice (5)	21/07/67★, 23/04/68, 04/06/68, 16/07/68, 24/10/68 Notorious for burning the Stars and Stripes at the Albert Hall, they started as the backing band for P.P. Arnold. Organist Keith Emerson formed Supergroup ELP with Greg Lake (King Crimson) and Carl Palmer (Chris Farlowe inter alia)

Night-Timers (21)	10/08/64+ ,02/08/64 with Dickie Pride, 21/07/64, 31/08/64+, 09/10/64+, 10/11/64, 30/11/64+, 11/01/65+, 09/02/65, 27/04/65, 18/05/65, 24/06/65★, 22/07/65★, 19/08/65★, 21/10/65★, 10/11/65, 26/05/66★, 28/07/66★, 13/10/66, 21/05/68, 19/06/69★ Spin-off from Georgie Fame
Nepenthé & the Jigsaw Band	02/05/68★
O'Hara's Playboys (4)	11/04/67, 04/01/68★, 15/02/68★, 30/07/68
Otis Spann	08/07/69
Paul Williams	06/02/69
Peter Bardens (2)	20/01/66★, 17/03/66★ with Rod Stewart
P.P. Arnold (2)	25/04/66, 16/06/67 with her backing band The Nice
Quintessence	06/01/70
Ram Jam Band with Geno Washington (16)	06/07/65, 26/08/65★, 28/10/65★, 04/11/65★, 18/11/65★, 25/11/65★, 16/12/65★, 06/01/66★, 27/01/66★, 13/01/66★, 03/02/66★, 10/02/66★, 24/02/66★, 19/04/66, 07/06/66, 27/09/66 High-octane club shows earned them a record contract and minor chart hits
Ray King Soul Band (2)	15/06/67★, 17/08/67★
Rebel Rousers	03/10/68★ They had just 'invited' Cliff Bennett to leave his own band
Riot Squad	20/03/69★
Rock n Roll Revival Show	09/04/68
Ronnie Jones (11)	22/12/64, 15/07/65★, 07/09/65, 21/12/65, 01/10/66, 20/12/66, 24/01/67, 28/03/67, 08/06/67★, 21/11/67, 11/01/68★
Root & Jenny Jackson (3)	05/10/67★, 07/11/68★, 05/06/69★

Roy C.	14/06/66 When requested to sing he didn't know his hit single, so who was he really?
Roy Harper (3)	10/12/68, 11/11/69, 13/01/70
Rufus Thomas	16/12/64 – Weds, backed by The Chessmen
Sam Apple Pie	**06/11/69★ the last Thursday at Klooks Kleek**
Sam the Sham	12/06/69★
Savoy Brown (9)	26/01/67★, 06/04/67★, 09/01/68, 12/03/68, 25/06/68, 10/09/68, 03/12/68 with Bobby Parker, 17/06/69, 25/11/69
Selofane	27/06/68★
Scotts of St James	02/02/67★
The Senate	09/08/66
The Sharrons	11/07/68★
The Shevelles (4)	02/09/65★, 14/04/66★, 15/09/66★, 04/07/68★
Shotgun Express (2)	16/08/66, 27/12/66 Line-up included Peter Green, Mick Fleetwood, Peter Bardens (*see* above) and Rod Stewart
Simon K. (2)	13/03/69★, 22/05/69★
Solomon Burke	19/07/66
Sonny Boy Williamson (2)	27/10/64 with The Moody Blues 05/01/65 with T-Bones
Sonny Childe & TNT	23/02/67★
Soul Sisters (2)	03/06/65★ with Brian Auger Trinity, 03/01/67/ with Tonicks
Soul Trinity (2)	06/07/67★, 31/08/67★
Spooky Tooth	06/08/68

The Steampacket (5)	05/10/65, 11/01/66, 15/02/66, 12/04/66, 06/09/66 Brought together Long John Baldry, Julie Driscoll, Rod Stewart and Brian Auger. Guitarist Vic Briggs also played with Eric Burdon's band, and drummer Mickey Waller with a host of others that included Beck, Berry, Fame, Hendrix, Jagger, Mayall and Penniman (Little Richard). If the term Supergroup had been invented at the time, it could have applied to The Steampacket
Stevie Wonder	01/02/66 with Sidewinders Still billed at the time as Little Stevie Wonder
The Strawbs	07/01/70 The Strawberry Hill Boys folkies changed tack just in time to play Klooks! Line-up included Rick Wakeman, later of Yes and immense solo success
Sugar Pie DeSanto	03/08/65 with The Shevelles
The Taste (2)	18/04/69★, 16/09/69★ The first Irish group at Klooks, with powerful guitarist Rory Gallagher
T-Bone Walker (2)	09/03/65 backed by John Mayall 19/10/65 backed by The Blue Jays
Ten Years After (4)	23/01/68, 27/02/68, 14/05/68 live recording at KK of the album *Undead*; 27/08/68 They had an ace guitarist called Alvin Lee, who was confused by many with Albert Lee (see Chris Farlowe in Top Billing). Alvin left the band in the '70s, and died in March 2013. TYA are still touring Europe and the States today
Terry Reid	29/04/69
T.H.E. Cat	27/07/67★

Tim Rose	01/10/68
Time Box (4)	04/04/68★, 09/05/68★, 29/08/68★, 30/01/69★
Tonicks (3)	23/03/67★, 28/09/67★ with Joey Young, 23/11/67★
Tony Colton	26/01/65
Trifle (2)	29/05/69★, 14/08/69★
Vagabonds (2)	15/03/66, 21/06/66 Evolved into Jimmy James, as above
Van de Graaf Generator	22/04/69
Village	09/10/69★
Warren Davis	21/03/68★ Merged into Happy Magazine, as above
The Web (7)	14/09/67★, 19/10/67★, 30/11/67★, 18/01/68★, 07/03/68★, 16/05/68★, 12/12/69★ (*see* John L Watson above)
Wellington Kitch	14/11/68★
Wes Minster 5 (6)	24/09/63, 15/10/63, 12/11/63, 03/12/63, 04/02/64, 28/04/64 One of the three bands rotating billing in the first four months of Klooks Kleek's R&B nights. Georgie Fame and Graham Bond were the others. Members of WM5 included Zoot Money, Jon Hiseman and Dave Greenslade, with Chris Farlowe as vocals. Later in bands such as Colosseum and Greenslade
William Bell	08/08/68★ backed by The Quotations
Wynder K Frogg	15/12/66★

Zoot Money and The Big Roll Band (34)	03/03/64, 17/03/64, 14/04/64, 20/04/64+, 05/05/64, 26/05/64, 01/06/64+, 16/06/64, 06/07/64+, 28/07/64, 15/09/64, 20/10/64, 21/12/64+, 25/01/65+, 08/03/65+, 01/04/65*, 06/05/65*, 08/06/65, 31/08/65, 28/09/65, 09/11/65, 31/12/65* **KK's highest-ever attendance**, 18/01/66, 22/02/66, 26/04/66, 31/05/66 **live recording of the album 'Zoot!'**, 12/07/66, 30/08/66, 18/10/66, 06/12/66, 21/02/67, 09/05/67, 03/10/67, 10/12/69-Weds One of the most popular performers at Klooks. The gap between 1967 and the final gig is explained by the band having morphed into Dantalian's Chariot, a psychedelic 20-minute solos band, before returning to their more popular R&B mode. Still working today, Zoot tours under his own name and participates in other projects

R&B, Blues and Rock Bands Playing the Interval at Klooks Kleek

(Top of the bill bands (totb) in bold type.)

Aardvark (3)	Graduated to 1 totb gig
Artwoods (11)	Graduated to 9 totbs 1964-65
Audience	
The Ax	
Barbarians & Prince Khan	
Bill Ashton (3)	The National Youth Jazz Orchestra founder who also liked to boogie
Bill's Bluesers	
Blues Healers (2)	
Bobo Links (3)	
Brothers Grimm	

Bulldog Breed	
Chessmen (7)	Graduated to 5 totbs and backing Rufus Thomas
Chicken Shack	4 totbs. 27/06/67 was singer Christine Perfect's first pro gig. Two years later, 'I would rather go blind', was a Number 1 chart hit. She joined Fleetwood Mac; the band earned steadily in Europe through the '70s
C Jam Blues	
Cliff Charles	
Cressida	
The Detroits	
The Dillingers (3)	
The Dissatisfieds (2)	
Distant Jim	
Dry Ice	
Duster Bennett	
East of Eden	1 totb
Egg (2)	Progressive jazz/rock, they didn't achieve same public notice as e.g., Soft Machine, Kevin Ayers
Elias Hulk	
Elysium	
Entire Sioux Nation	Off-putting on space grounds
Fat John Band (4)	
Felder's Orioles	2 totbs
The Fingernail 5	
For Ever More	
Gordon Smith	
Gracious	
Gun	Had a hit single, 'Race with the Devil'
Gun Hill	
Hard Meat	2 totbs
High Tide	
Hogsnort Rupert & his good band	

Jan Dukes de Grey	
Jimmie Williamson	
Jody Grind	
John Cole Rubies	
John Gummer Quartet (10)	
John James (2)	
John Thomas (3)	
Julian's Treatment	
Junco Partners (2)	
Junior's Eyes (2)	8 totbs
Kiko Six (2)	
Killing Floor	
Kingsnakes (2)	
Legay	
Lester Square and the GT's	
Lucas and the Emperors	
Lucifer	
Magic Horse	
Mastersounds	
Mighty Baby	After being totb
Milestones	
The Mojos	
The Moody Blues	Played Klooks on 29/09/64 before becoming one of the leading stadium rock bands of the late 1960s and '70s, they were here promoting their first single and Number 1 hit, 'Go Now'. Fee 30*s* (£1.50)
My Cake	
Nite People	
Nozepickers	
The Outsiders (5)	
Porky and the Pies (5)	
Ray Warley (2)	
The Roosters	
Rumble and Sonja	
Samson	**Played the very last interval**

Savoy Brown Blues Band (4)	9 totbs and good earnings in US/English boom
Second Thoughts (3)	
Seventh Sun	
Shakey Vic (2)	
Sisyphus	… found it a bit of a struggle
Sleepy	
Spice (2)	
The Steamhammer	
Steve Miller	No, not that one!
Stormsville Shakers	
Stray (2)	
The Termites	
Terry Reid	1 totb
Tom Jones Ltd (4)	Not that one!
Tony Colton	1 totb
Truck	
Union Blues	
Van de Graaf Generator	1 totb
Victor Brox Blues Train	
Welcome	
The Wes Minster 5	Their swan-song after 6 totbs
The Wishbones	
Wishbone Ash	Started too late to feature at Klooks; went on to a dozen years of album success

Modern Jazz Artists Topping the Bill at Klooks Kleek

Alan Skidmore – tenor sax (3)	15/11/61, 28/03/62, 01/05/63, With his dad, Jimmy, on tenor sax
Art Ellefson – tenor sax (7)	19/07/61, 13/06/62, 08/08/62, 02/01/63, 06/11/63, 06/05/64 with fellow tenorist Danny Moss, 30/09/64 with trumpeter Kenny Wheeler
Baron Marsh Sextet	05/07/61

Barry Kerswell Sextet	12/04/61
Bert Courtley – trumpet (6)	21/02/62, 29/08/62, 12/12/62, 19/06/63, 30/10/63, 22/07/64, with tenor saxist Kathy Stobart
Bill LeSage – piano, vibes (8)	25/01/61, 15/02/61, 26/07/61, 23/05/62, 10/10/62, 13/03/63, 08/05/63, 25/09/63 with Dave Morse
Bob Efford – tenor sax (2)	25/04/62, 27/05/64 with tenor saxist Tommy Whittle Bob only topped the bill twice but was at the club every other week for 'a blow'
Bobby Breen – singer (5)	14/10/64 with tenor saxist Dick Morrissey, 21/10/64 with tenor saxist Danny Moss, 28/10/64 with Dick Morrissey, 04/11/64 with Danny Moss, 11/11/64 with Dick Morrissey
Bobby Wellins	17/10/62
Brian Auger Trinity (2)	07/08/63 with trumpeter Mike Falana, 18/12/63 with Tommy Whittle and singer Jo Stahl
Clive Burrows Octet	07/06/61
Colin Peters Quartet	14/11/62
Danny Moss – tenor sax (8)	08/03/61, 27/12/61, 11/12/63 & 19/02/64 with Dave Castle, 08/04/64 with baritone saxist Ronnie Ross, 06/05/64 with Art Ellefson, 09/09/64 with the Eddie Thompson trio, 07/10/64 with Tommy Whittle (*see* Bobby Bree)
Dave Castle – saxes (2)	11/12/63, 19/02/64 with Danny Moss

Dave Morse Quintet (12)	20/09/61, 22/11/61, 06/12/61, 24/01/62, 14/02/62, 14/03/62, 04/04/62, 02/05/62, 05/12/62, 27/02/63 25/09/63 solo with Bill LeSage, also solo 18/04/64 Official Jam Session
Dick Morrissey – tenor sax (20)	18/01/61, 29/03/61, 02/08/61 with flautist Johnny Scott, 06/09/61 with vibes player Lennie Best, 10/05/63, 19/12/62, 20/02/63, 03/04/63, 22/05/63, 03/07/63, 04/09/63, 02/10/63 with singer Jo Stahl, 20/11/63 withThe Morrissey-Ian Bird Sextet, 01/01/64 with trumpeter Gus Galbraith, 22/01/64, 01/04/64 with valve-trombonist Ken Wray, 11/03/64 with Jo Stahl, 13/05/64 with baritone saxist Harry Klein, 29/07/64 with baritone saxist Glen Hughes, 23/09/64 with Bobby Breen
Dick Heckstall-Smith – tenor	15/08/62 Later featured in several R&B bands, and as he lived round the corner from the club, jammed regularly with whoever was appearing
Don Rendell – tenor sax (19)	**11/01/61 Opening night of Klooks Kleek**, 05/04/61, 28/06/61, 04/10/61, 07/02/62, 30/05/62, 01/08/62, 12/09/62 with Graham Bond, 07/11/62, 06/02/63, 24/04/63, 05/06/63 with the Don Rendell Quartet, 31/07/63, 11/09/63 with trumpeter Kenny Baker, 29/01/64 with the Don Rendell Quintet, 04/03/64 with Harry Klein, 18/04/64 official jam session, 29/04/64 with Tommy Whittle, 03/06/64, 02/09/64 with trumpeter Ian Carr

Duncan Lamont – tenor	12/08/64 with Johnny Scott
Eddie Thompson – piano	09/09/64 with Danny Moss
Fat John Band	15/01/64
Geoff Rideout	21/06/61
Georgie Fame	21/08/63
Glen Hughes – baritone sax (3)	18/09/63, 24/06/64, 29/07/64, with Dick Morrissey A regular unscheduled gigger, his forceful style brought him many fans. Famously 'battled' the top man Ronnie Ross one evening; Ronnie was generous in his praise. Glen was later in Georgie Fame's band on several of the hits. Sadly, dead before he was 30
Graham Bond – alto sax (4)	28/02/62 & 12/09/62 with Don Rendell, tenor sax 17/04/63 & 26/06/63 the Graham Bond quartet
Gus Galbraith – trumpet (3)	01/01/64 with Dick Morrissey, 18/04/64 Jam Session, 12/02/65 the Gus Galbraith Quintet
Harold McNair – alto sax	11/10/61 Ultra-cool Jamaican saxist
Harry Klein – baritone (3)	12/06/63, 23/10/63 & 04/03/64 with Don Rendell
Helen May	19/04/61
Ian Bird Quintet	09/08/61
Ian Carr – trumpet (2)	16/10/63 with Don Rendell, 18/04/64 jam session
Jimmy Deuchar – trumpet	01/03/61
Jimmy Skidmore – tenor sax (10)	15/11/61 with son Alan, 27/06/62 05/09/62 with wife Kathy Stobart, 24/10/62, 26/12/62, 01/05/63 with Alan, 24/07/63, 04/12/63 with vibraphonist Lennie Best 20/05/63 with Ken Wray, 18/04/64 Official Jam Session

Jo Stahl – singer (3)	02/10/63 with Dick Morrissey, 18/12/63 with Brian Auger Trinity, 11/03/64 with Dick Morrissey
Joe Harriott – alto sax (6)	18/04/62, 23/01/63, 28/08/63 with trumpeter Shake Keane on 27/11/63, 05/02/64, 25/03/64
John Burch Octet (4)	30/01/63, 20/03/63, 10/06/64, 15/07/64 John, piano, arranger/composer, recruited inter alia Ginger Baker, Graham Bond, Jack Bruce, Dick Heckstall-Smith and worked with visiting US jazz stars. Also wrote the B-side for Georgie Fame's Number 1 hit, 'Yeh, Yeh'
Johnnie Mumford	04/07/62
Johnny Scott – flute (6)	08/02/61, 02/08/61 with Dick Morrissey, 29/11/61, 31/01/62, 22/04/62, 12/08/64 with Duncan Lamont
John West Group (2)	18/10/61, 10/01/62
John Williams 9tette (2)	14/08/63, 09/10/63 with the Big Band
Kathy Stobart – tenor sax (4)	31/05/61, 07/03/62, 05/09/62 with her husband, Jimmy Skidmore, 22/07/64 with trumpeter Bert Courtley
Keith Christie – trombone (5)	01/02/61, 22/03/61, 24/05/61, 25/10/61, 08/07/64 with Ken Wray
Ken Wray – valve trombone (5)	22/01/64, 01/04/64 with Dick Morrissey, 08/07/64 with Keith Christie, 19/08/64 with Tommy Whittle, 18/04/64 official jam session
Kenny Baker – trumpet	01/07/64 with Tommy Whittle While widely known as a mainstream bandleader and soloist on radio and TV, but he never forgot his jazz roots

Kenny Wheeler – trumpet	30/09/64 A surprising single appearance for a much-admired player. His obligations to Johnny Dankworth's band probably explain it
Lennie Best – vibraphone (5)	26/04/61, 14/06/61, 06/09/61 with Dick Morrissey, 08/11/61, 04/12/63 with Jimmy Skidmore
Mike Falana – trumpet	07/08/63 with Brian Auger Trinity
Milton James Sextet	29/05/63
Pete King – alto, tenor sax	12/07/61 Not to be confused with Peter King of Ronnie Scott fame
The Polish Modern Jazz Quartet (2)	26/08/64, 16/09/64 (by acclaim)
Red Price – saxes and organ	22/04/64 with Sandy Brown
Ronnie Ross – baritone sax (11)	15/03/61, 03/05/61, 27/09/61, 13/12/61, 11/04/62, 20/06/62, 19/09/62 with Jimmy Skidmore, 16/01/63, 10/04/63, 17/07/63, 08/04/64 with Danny Moss Ronnie became the doyen of British baritone saxists in succession to Harry Klein. Wider public fame came much later in the form of his typically cool solo on Lou Reed's 1973 hit single 'Walk on the Wild Side'
Roy East – alto and flute (3)	13/09/61, 28/11/62, 06/03/63 with Tony Russell
Sandy Brown – clarinet (2)	17/01/62, 22/04/64 with Red Price One of the post-war trad-jazz revivalists who was a prime influence in the move to mainstream jazz. His McJazz recording with trumpeter Al Fairweather is regarded by many as historic
Shake Keane – trumpet (3)	27/11/63, 05/02/64, 25/03/64 with Joe Harriott. Shake's lively style combined wonderfully with Joe's cool tones

Six Sounds	26/02/64
Stan Robinson – tenor (2)	21/03/62, 06/06/62
Ted Leach	17/05/61
Tommy Whittle – tenor (14)	16/08/61, 03/01/62, with Les Carlton on 16/05/62, 11/07/62, 26/09/62, 15/05/63,10/07/63, 18/09/63 with Glen Hughes, 13/11/63, 29/04/64 with Don Rendell, 27/05/64 with Bob Efford, 01/07/64 with Kenny Baker, 19/05/64 with Ken Wray, 07/10/64 with Danny Moss Tommy was one of the best-known jazzmen of the '50s and '60s. Ran his own club night in a pub in not-too-distant Wembley, happily on a Thursday!
Tony Coe – alto (2)	25/07/62, 21/11/62
Tony Russell – trombone (2)	28/11/62, 06/03/63 with Roy East
Tubby Hayes – tenor, baritone, flute, vibraphone etc (7)	01/11/61, 31/10/62, 09/01/63 with the Tubby Hayes Quintet, 13/06/63 with the Quartet, 08/01/64 with the Quintet, 15/04/64 with the Quintet, 17/06/64 with the Quintet
Vic Ash – clarinet, soprano sax (6)	22/02/61, 30/08/61, 20/12/61, 09/05/62, 18/07/62, 27/03/63 with the Wally Houser Quintet
Wally Houser – alto (2)	27/03/63 (his Quintet) with Vic Ash 18/03/64 official jam session Wally, a practising solicitor (in which profession he was most definitely Walter), led the house backing group for a couple of years

Modern Jazz Artists Playing the Interval at Klooks Kleek (01/1961 to 11/1964)

B.U.D. Quintet
Budricos
Chris Pine Quintet

Claude Laugier	
Colin Peters (piano) Trio (3)	
Dave Duval Trinity	
Dave Watkins Quartet	
Derek Sutton Trio (6)	
Jazz Confessors	A quintet led by Tony Baylis
Jim Douglas Quartet	
Jim Douglas Quintet	
Lionel Grigson 7 (2)	
Marc Blackburn Quartet (3)	
Mike Osborne Quintet (2)	
Mike Westbrook Big Band	
Mike Westbrook Quintet (2)	In the '70s Mike became one of the best-known composers and performers (piano) of progressive jazz
Milton James 7	Topped the bill a month later
Ned Bray Quartet (22)	
Pete Lemer Quartet	
Red Bludd's Bluesicians	The band included Bill Ashton, Jon Lord, Art Wood
Ted Beament Trio	
Tony Baylis (36)	Bassist Tony played modern jazz, trad jazz (Alex Welsh) and R&B (Long John Baldry, Rod Stewart), working in numerous other bands over the years

Modern Jazz Artists Topping the Bill at Dopey Dick's (1967/68)

Afro-Cubists	21/06/67 (*see* Kenny Graham)
Al Cohn - tenor	06/09/67 with Zoot Sims and Stan Tracey
Alan Haven Duo (2)	03/05/67, 19/07/67 Organist Alan with Tony Crombie on the drums

Alvin Roy's Jazz Band	03/07/68 (a one-off trad jazz event)
Annie Ross – singer	23/08/67 with the Harry South Trio Annie had returned to UK after achieving fame with Dave Lambert and Jon Hendricks
Ben Webster – tenor sax (2)	19/04/67 with the John Patrick Trio 04/10/67 with the Pat Smythe Trio
Blossom Dearie – piano	28/06/67
Bob Stuckey (piano) Trio (2)	17/04/68, 24/04/68 **the last regular evening for Dopey Dick's**
Brian Auger – piano/organ Trinity (2)	14/02/68, 10/04/68
Buck Clayton – trumpet	12/04/67 with John Chilton
Bud Johnson	25/10/67
Clouds	20/03/68
Coleman Hawkins – tenor	22/11/67
Dakota Staton – singer	12/07/67 with the Pete King Quartet
Dick Morrissey (tenor) Quartet (2)	17/05/67. Also 02/08/67 supporting Mark Murphy
Don Rendell (tenor)/ Ian Carr Quintet (3)	07/06/67, 16/08/67, 01/11/67
Eddie 'Lockjaw' Davis – tenor	**05/04/67 opening session** with the Harold McNair Quartet
Graham Bond – alto, organ (5)	07/02/68, 21/02/68, 28/02/68, 06/03/68, 13/03/68
Graham Collier Dozen	30/08/67 One of the stalwarts of British jazz, bassist Graham established himself as a composer, arranger and music educator in later years
Harold McNair (alto) Quartet (2)	05/04/67 (returning to the club after 6 years in support of 'Lockjaw' Davis), 24/05/67

Harry South – piano	23/08/67 backing Annie Ross Harry had his own big band which made a classic album with Georgie Fame. Moved into film and TV and wrote the theme tune to *The Sweeney*
Ian Carr (trumpet)/ Don Rendell Quintet (3)	07/06/67, 16/08/67, 01/11/67
Jimmy McGriff (organ) Quartet (2)	24/01/68, 29/10/68 **the last-ever jazz event at Dopey Dick's**
Joe Harriott (alto) Quintet	31/05/67
Kenny Graham – tenor	27/09/67 Played in numerous bands to pay the bills without ever losing his great love for Afro-Cuban jazz. He celebrated the 1951 Festival of Britain with a 78rpm, 'Skylon' and 'Dome of Discovery'
London Youth Jazz Orchestra	26/07/67
Mark Murphy – singer (2)	10/05/67 with Pat Smythe Trio, 02/08/67 with the Dick Morrissey Quartet
Matt Ross – piano, organ	05/07/67 with Mike Carr and Bob Stuckey
Max Roach Quintet	18/10/67 The master drummer needed no amplification
Mike Carr – organ, vibes (2)	05/07/67 with Bob Stuckey and Matt Ross, 08/11/67 with Tony Crombie
Pat Smythe – piano	10/05/67 with Mark Murphy
Pete Brown's Jazz & Poetry	03/04/68 Jack Bruce's co-composer of Cream hits had an original life as leading exponent of this form of jazz
Pete King - tenor	12/07/09 supporting Dakota Staton
Roland Kirk – tenor, alto, soprano, nose flute, and often at the same time	15/11/67

Ronnie Scott (tenor) – his quartet	11/10/67 The famous club owner, whose artistes filled the Dopey Dick's roster, then he got on the tube for his own gig
Sonny Rollins – tenor	26/04/67 with the Stan Tracey Trio
Stan Tracey – piano (2)	26/04/67 as preceding 06/09/67 with Zoot Sims and Al Cohn. Stan lived on the Kilburn High Road in the same building as Cleo Laine and Johnny Dankworth.
Ted Heath Orchestra	13/09/67 THO was where most of the British star soloists had learned the trade
Tony Crombie – drums (2)	03/05/67, 19/07/67 with Alan Haven Brilliant technique and not a little showmanship ensured his popularity
Tubby Hayes Quartet	14/06/67
Yusuf Lateef – flute and saxes	09/08/67 with Stan Jones Trio
Zoot Sims – tenor	06/09/67 with Al Cohn and the Stan Tracey Trio

Modern Jazz Artists Playing the Interval at Dopey Dick's (1967/68)

Bob Stuckey (piano) Quartet/ Trio (2)	2 totb
Brian Lemon (piano) Trio (2)	
Colin Purbrook Trio (18)	
Purbrook/Baldock/Cox (3)	Pianist (and anything else that needed playing) Colin, ex-Sandy Brown, ex-Don Rendell and accompanist to a host of US star soloists, lived round the corner from Klooks. Google Steve Voce's 1999 obit in the *Independent* to see how tremendous a character he was
Jeff Reed Trio (2)	
Kenny Baldock – bass (3)	With Colin Purbrook. Another Dankworth alumnus

Matt Ross – piano

Stan Jones

Terry Cox (3)	With Colin Purbrook, whose drummer Terry Cox knew from the Sandy Brown days

FURTHER READING

Louis Barfe (2004), *Where Have All the Good Times Gone? The Rise and Fall of the Record Industries*. Atlantic Books.

Bob Brunning (2002), *Blues: The British Connection*. Helter Skelter Publishing.

John Chilton (2004), *Who's Who of British Jazz*. Continuum.

Mark Cunningham (1998), *Good Vibrations: A History of Record Production*. Sanctuary Publishing.

John Fordham (1986), *Jazz Man: The Amazing Story of Ronnie Scott and his Club*. Kyle Cathie Limited.

Mo Foster (2000), *17 Watts? The Birth of British Rock Guitar*. MPG Books.

Pete Frame (1993), *Rock Family Trees*. Omnibus Press.

Pete Frame (2007), *The Restless Generation: How Rock Music Changed the Face of 1950s Britain*. Rogan House.

Jim Godbolt (1989), *A History of Jazz in Britain, 1950 to 1970*. Quartet Books.

Martyn Hanson, edited by Colin Richardson (2010), *Playing the Band – The Musical Life of Jon Hiseman*. Temple Music.

Dick Heckstall-Smith and Pete Grant (2004), *Blowing the Blues: Fifty Years of Playing British Blues*. Clear Books.

Christopher Hjort (2007), *Strange Brew: Eric Clapton and the British Blues Boom*. Jawbone Press.

Andrew Loog Oldham (2001), *Stoned*. Vintage.

Andrew Loog Oldham (2003), 2*Stoned*. Vintage.

Paul M. Pelletier (1984), *Decca Complete Singles Catalogue 1954 to 1983*. Record Information Services.

Johnny Rogan (1988), *Starmakers and Svengalis*. Queen Anne Press, Macdonald & Co.

Harry Shapiro (2005), *Graham Bond: The Mighty Shadow*. The Crossroads Press.

Harry Shapiro (2010), *Jack Bruce: Composing Himself*. Outline Press.

Gordon Thompson (2008), *Please Please Me*. Oxford Press.

Chris Welch (2000), *Cream: The Legendary Sixties Supergroup*. Balafon Books, Outline Press.